**SpringerBriefs in Well-Being and Quality
of Life Research**

SpringerBriefs in Well-Being and Quality-of-Life Research are concise summaries of cutting-edge research and practical applications across the field of well-being and quality of life research. These compact refereed monographs are under the editorial supervision of an international Advisory Board*. Volumes are 50 to 125 pages (approximately 20,000–70,000 words), with a clear focus. The series covers a range of content from professional to academic such as: snapshots of hot and/or emerging topics, in-depth case studies, and timely reports of state-of-the art analytical techniques. The scope of the series spans the entire field of Well-Being Research and Quality-of-Life Studies, with a view to significantly advance research. The character of the series is international and interdisciplinary and will include research areas such as: health, cross-cultural studies, gender, children, education, work and organizational issues, relationships, job satisfaction, religion, spirituality, ageing from the perspectives of sociology, psychology, philosophy, public health and economics in relation to Well-being and Quality-of-Life research. Volumes in the series may analyze past, present and/or future trends, as well as their determinants and consequences. Both solicited and unsolicited manuscripts are considered for publication in this series. SpringerBriefs in Well-Being and Quality-of-Life Research will be of interest to a wide range of individuals with interest in quality of life studies, including sociologists, psychologists, economists, philosophers, health researchers, as well as practitioners across the social sciences. Briefs will be published as part of Springer's eBook collection, with millions of users worldwide. In addition, Briefs will be available for individual print and electronic purchase. Briefs are characterized by fast, global electronic dissemination, standard publishing contracts, easy-to-use manuscript preparation and formatting guidelines, and expedited production schedules. We aim for publication 8–12 weeks after acceptance.

More information about this series at http://www.springer.com/series/10150

Gareth Davey

Quality of Life and Well-Being in an Indian Ethnic Community

The Case of Badagas

 Springer

Gareth Davey
School of Anthropology and Conservation
The University of Kent
Canterbury, Kent
UK

ISSN 2211-7644   ISSN 2211-7652   (electronic)
SpringerBriefs in Well-Being and Quality of Life Research
ISBN 978-3-319-90661-4   ISBN 978-3-319-90662-1   (eBook)
https://doi.org/10.1007/978-3-319-90662-1

Library of Congress Control Number: 2018939310

Printed on acid-free paper

This Springer imprint is published by the registered company Springer International Publishing AG
part of Springer Nature
The registered company address is: Gewerbestrasse 11, 6330 Cham, Switzerland

Contents

Introduction

Abstract This chapter introduces Badagas, an ethnic minority in India, and their general portrayal by scholars. Drawing on literature since the colonial era, it reviews different representations, collectively a social construction of a distinct cultural and ethnic identity category for a specific population and way of life—a popular imagination of a hill tribe in a remote region bound by strong ties to ancient myths and rituals, kinship, and land. Colonists, missionaries, and early intellectuals gave the false appearance of coherence to people in othering and social boundary-making processes, a mindset grounded in European colonial expansion and early anthropology. Later writers uncritically adopted and reinscribed a reified identity through detailed investigations of its defining criteria, and in this way misleading stereotypes have been stamped in the literature over many years. Another aim of the chapter is to pinpoint what is already known about Badagas, as well as gaps in knowledge, to make a case for the empirical research reported in this book which is a multi-sited ethnography of life quality and identities among Badagas in two connected locations, the first online among Internet forum users, and the second in the real world with rural-to-urban migrants in Bangalore.

Keywords Badagas · Identity · Nilgiri Hills · Quality of life

The Nilgiri Hills rise majestically on the plains of South India as a picturesque landscape cloaked by greenish-blue mist and blossoming purple flowers. They are well known to social scientists as the location of over a dozen indigenous communities, which have long been an object of academic attention. Badagas are the numerically largest ethnic minority group. This book is about their experiences as they navigate a society in flux, and the extent to which modernity permeates life. It is a timely update of previous in-depth research on Badagas, and an important case study of the impact of the country's economic and social development on its people. Badagas, like everyone in India, have been experiencing profound changes as new ways of living have become widespread. For example, an increasing number of people are migrating to cities in search of employment, and using technologies such as new media, which are influencing how they live, grounded on broader shifts in Indian society.

G. Davey, *Quality of Life and Well-Being in an Indian Ethnic Community*,
SpringerBriefs in Well-Being and Quality of Life Research,
https://doi.org/10.1007/978-3-319-90662-1_1

1

The primary concern of my research is an investigation of the life quality and identities of Badagas with reference to rural-to-urban migration and new media. At an empirical level, this monograph unpacks how they understand and embrace life to the full in the twenty-first century. However, it also challenges ways they have been understood and portrayed in the literature. At a theoretical level, then, it charts the historical formation of the identity category, deconstructs epistemological claims about its meaning for a specific population, and rebalances inequalities of representation. Thus the book is a critical appraisal of previous writings combined with fresh thinking about quality of life and the ambiguities and paradoxies of contemporary identities at work.

To set the scene, this chapter introduces Badagas in the Nilgiri Hills and their general portrayal by scholars, to tease out some of the themes and styles which characterise writings. The following sections draw on literature since the colonial era to show how the category 'Badaga' is primarily a reified social-political construct advocated by colonists, missionaries, and early intellectuals who gave the false appearance of coherence to people and their identities and quality of life. I also hope to weave an argument more complicated than claiming that it is merely an invention of the British, by analysing its construction by social actors and historical and political processes in India. The following sections also critically discuss the numerous criteria typically used to characterise Badagas, based on assumptions by previous writers that they share a common history and culture, and show the literature does not fully do justice to the diversity of ways people interpret being Badaga; similarly, as the research is also about their quality of life, the chapter delineates its documentation, and reveals it has similarly been shaped by complex historical, political, and social forces. Finally, another aim is to pinpoint what is already known about Badagas, as well as gaps in knowledge, to make a case for the empirical research reported in Chapters "Badagas Going Digital" and "Migrants' Voices".

Once upon a Time: The Beginnings

The earliest recorded descriptions of the Nilgiri Hills date to the second century BCE in *Srimad Valmiki Ramayana*, an ancient Sanskrit epic poem which narrates the journey of the Hindu Sage Valmiki, and to 1572 and *Os Lusíadas*, an epic poem of Portuguese voyages during the fifteenth and sixteenth centuries by Luís Vaz de Camões (Hockings 2008). Archeological studies in the Nilgiri Hills have produced prehistoric material such as rock art and stone structures, but it is not known if they are connected to the indigenous people (Breeks 1873; Congreve 1847; Zagarell 1997).

The earliest written account of the local population was in 1603 by the Italian Jesuit priest Jacome Ferreira from the Syrian Church of Malabar. He is styled in the literature as the first European to set foot in the Nilgiri Hills while searching for villages of ancient Christians of the St. Thomas Christian community, although his church had previously dispatched others to the hills to collect information about the local people (Whitehouse 1873). Ferreira documented his journey and observations of people in the hills such as their lifestyles, population sizes, and settlements (Rivers 1906; Whitehouse 1873), the first known account of a topic which does not appear in the literature again until the nineteenth century when adventurers, civil servants, and missionaries in British India published censuses, district gazetteers, reports, and travel writings (Breeks 1873; Francis 1908; Grigg 1880; Thurston and Rangachari 1909). These early representations of Badagas were penned in a style characteristic of colonists and missionaries prior to the development of social science in the twentieth century. Exploration of the New World by Europeans in the 18th and 19th centuries meant that strange and exciting cultures began to be reported back in Europe, which fueled a curiosity among intellectuals and the upper classes. Colonialism and missionary activities brought Europeans—who regarded themselves as 'civilized', 'modern', and 'advanced'—into contact with people whose appearances, beliefs, customs, and ways of life were regarded as exotic and primitive, based on the premise that indigenous cultures were facing extinction. In this context, people in the Nilgiri Hills were described as separate and peculiar with distinct and striking physical appearances, notions of backward primitive tribes associated with the jungle.

Thus, the category emerged as a social construct out of othering and social boundary-making processes based on ideas and material relations in European colonial expansion and imperialism, a social construction which in part legitimised colonial rule in India as it portrayed the Indian population as in need of being governed. The Indian population was subdivided into different 'castes', 'classes, 'races', and 'tribes', an emphasis of marked difference to British writers and each other. As there is disagreement and inconsistency in the literature concerning the categorisation of Badagas as a caste, tribe or other group, and the Nilgiri Hills as a caste or tribal society (Hockings 1968, 1993; Mahias 1997), these terms are used loosely in this monograph only to highlight styles and trends in previous writings (and with no implied meanings such as perceived cultural or economic backwardness). Even so, the opinion that Badagas constitute a caste is central to identity and quality of life. Hockings (1968, 1988, 1993) speculated that Badagas were very much aware of their distinctiveness as a caste by having their own language, culture, and oral tradition about their ancestors' migration from the former Mysore region. He also reported that they identified themselves as Backward Class (an official classification conferred by the Indian government), and therefore as 'culturally superior to, or not as primitive as' the socially disadvantaged Scheduled Tribes (Kotas, Todas, and Kurumbas) in the Nilgiri Hills. Other distinctions Hockings thought they were aware of included same-caste marriage based on endogamy, the practice of marrying within a specific group; ritual purity and impurity, which forbid intimate relations and marriage with other ethnic groups; dress and tilaka; birth and residence in recognised hamlets (assemblages of villages, each with several hundred inhabitants); and the ability of two people of the same phratry (subcaste) to trace a tentative kinship connection. However, it has also been argued that Badagas did not fit the typical caste model prevalent in South India as their ancestors were migrants and separated from caste society (Hockings 1980a, 1982). While Badagas have been categorised as a caste by some writers, it is a highly contested category as a product of two hundred years of British domination which made it the central symbol of Indian society (Dirks 2001), and the nuances of the label from Badagas themselves have not been studied. It may no longer convey the sense of community that it once did, but 'caste' is still a primary form of local identification for many people in India, and remains a signifier of India's diverse forms of identities, a core feature of social organization even in serious critique of the concept.

Serious academic research began in the twentieth century onwards. W. H. R. Rivers in 1906 wrote about the kinship and social organization of Todas, now a classic for its novel approach to ethnography which later became standard practice in British social anthropology (Hockings 2008; Rivers 1906). Murray Emeneau and David Mandelbaum conducted seminal works on Kota and Toda languages (Emeneau 1944–46, 1989; Mandelbaum 1941). Like many Indian ethnic groups documented in social science, Badagas also have a classic ethnographer and then followers who take up particular issues. This role was filled by Paul Hockings who conducted doctoral studies on Badagas at the University of California, Berkeley in the 1960s. He devoted a large part of his distinguished career to Badagas, and his books and articles have painstakingly recorded the intricacies of their way of life as well as the cultural ecology of the Nilgiri Hills. However, much of his work including recent books (Hockings 1999, 2013) is based on fieldwork conducted up to the 1990s. Other scholars have published short reports, but Badagas remain neglected in academic literature. Even so, an army of scholars have since marched over the Nilgiri Hills from almost every possible research angle, and a recent innovation has been an interdisciplinary interest—architecture, climate, human geography, and zoology, to name a few foci.

Unfortunately, a great deal of writings are based on old-fashioned notions of small-scale and isolated societies with exotic and traditional lifestyles, and reflect the succession of ideological positions in early social science including evolutionism, diffusionism, and functionalism. Later writers uncritically adopted and reinscribed the reification of coherent identity categories with detailed investigations of stereo-typical criteria which they thought differentiated them. These include, for example, community, customs and rituals, economy, folk medicine, history, kinship, language, and religion, markers of similarity and difference which all correspond to and complement one another in a common cultural space. On this basis, authors have tended to separate Badagas in simple and crude terms such as "there is hardly any doubt as to who is and is not a Badaga...they constitute a distinct community linguistically, culturally, and socially" (Heidemann 2014, p. 94), and "the community is a grouping where potential membership is the same as actual membership, no problem arises in practice over who is a Badaga and who is not" (Hockings 1980a, p. 2). In this way, a simplified category ('Badagas' or 'Badaga community') has been stamped in the literature in the last century, a false appearance of coherence to a body of stereo-typical yardsticks that are actually complex and diverse. The next sections of this chapter overview some of these criteria to highlight the ways a distinct identity and quality of life have been portrayed and the limitations. The analysis is also relevant to critically reading writings on other ethnic minorities in the Nilgiris and India.

Migration and Identity

The history of Badagas has been separated from other people in the Nilgiri Hills, although no archeological or historical records have been discovered in support. Writers have stated Badagas did not exist until the arrival and consolidation of various migrant groups in the hills, events which are regarded as their beginnings (Hockings 1980a). Claims they were migrants are based on folk beliefs among Badagas of successive waves of migration in the sixteenth or seventeenth century by people of Vokkaliga castes from the southern plains of the former Mysore region; they were supposedly granted permission to settle in the Nilgiri Hills by Kotas, Kurumbas, and Todas (Benbow 1930; Emeneau 1944–1946; Francis 1908; Grigg 1880; Harkness 1832; Hockings 1980a, 1999; Thurston and Rangachari 1909). A well-cited Kota folk story recounts their meeting with the first migrants who pleaded for land upon arrival in the hills (Belli Gowder 1923–1941; Emeneau 1944–1946; Hockings 1980a). Epic ballads and legends retell stories of the origin and settlement of the migrant community including individuals and families thought to have founded specific villages. Several authors have published analyses of these stories (Benbow 1930; Francis 1908; Thurston and Rangachari 1909; Emeneau 1944–1946; Grigg 1880; Hockings 1980a). Notably, Hockings (1980a, 1988) examined in detail folk stories about intermittent migrations by ancestors of Badagas to shed light on places of origin, sequences of arrival, and formation of kinship and exogamy in newly-established villages, as some legends mention the beginnings of particular family lineages and villages. Other indigenous groups in the Nilgiri Hills have been described as having different origin myths about their creation locally by gods (Emeneau 1944–1946).

Some authors have attempted to date and explain the establishment of the Badaga community, although there have been accounts of several waves of migrations for different reasons (Belli Gowder 1938–1941; Emeneau 1944–1946; Harkness 1832; Hockings 1980a; Ward 1821). As some legends describe people fleeing Muslim soldiers, it has been reasoned the ancestors of Badagas departed their homeland due to political turmoil and oppression, for example during the invasion of Malik Kafur (Belli Gowder 1938–41) or The Battle of Talikota and subsequent destruction of the Vijayanagara Empire (Belli Gowder 1923–1941; Emeneau 1944–1946; Hockings 1980a, 1999). Some historians believe Muslim horsemen extorted money and goods from people after the fall of Vijayanagara, alongside robberies and plundering operations by gangs of warlords, events which concur with those retold in Badaga folklore. Kota folklore also claims Badagas fled to the Nilgiri Hills 'because of the trouble Mohammedan made for us...we have come, making ourselves to escape. This country is yours...we are helpless. You must help us' (Emeneau 1944–1946, p. 257; Hockings 1999, p. 28). Badaga folklore claims the first village established in the Nilgiri Hills was Tuneri; and the first settler became the head of the Badaga community, a hereditary position subsequently passed patrilineally from father to son. Hockings (1999) estimated the date of Tuneri's origin using family records (dates of birth) of previous headmen. As the incumbent headman at the time of his study was able to name nineteen generations of his family, Hockings counted back seventeen to eighteen generations to conclude the first headman might have been born around 1600 A.D., near the time of The Battle of Talikota.

However, these studies of oral tradition seem rudimentary at best. Also, folklore should be treated with caution as it is not necessarily based on actual events, and typically includes stories beyond the realm of possibility with magic and miracles. Therefore, it operates with uncertainty, never entirely believed by people but also never resolutely doubted. Even details of real events may be forgotten or miscommunicated as people do not always remember details accurately, not the best research method for obtaining data such as dates and places. Also, many localities in South Asia are associated with origin myths. While I appreciate folkloristics, the folkloric origin of the migration implies that academic research aiming to confirm its authenticity is misguided (perhaps on par with efforts by cryptozoologists who try to prove the existence of entities from the folklore record like Bigfoot or The Loch Ness Monster). Other anecdotal evidence cited in the literature is also unconvincing. Census and population data have been used to support a migration premise. According to the earliest known report, the population of Badagas was about 500 in only three villages in the seventeenth century (Ferreira 1603). The first rough British census in 1812 reported that Badagas numbered 2207 in 350 villages, suggesting by then they were the numerically-dominant indigenous group, as Todas numbered 179 and Kotas 130 (Hockings 1980a). While it has been suggested these data reflect community establishment and growth following migration (Hockings 1980a), the possibility of population growth in an indigenous population has been overlooked (it could also be that Ferreira's anecdotal observations are inaccurate). It is also not clear why those who might have fled the plains did not return (as was the case with other groups). That 'Badaga' means 'northener' in Badagu (the language of Badagas) has also been regarded as evidence for a migration to the Nilgiri Hills from the plains just to the north, first noted by Ferreira in 1603 (Hockings 1980a; Ward 1821); indeed, hamlets in the Badaga community are thought to have originated by settlers from villages with similar names in the former Mysore region (Hockings 1997). The proposition that Badagu is an archaic dialect of the Kannada spoken in Mysore has also been put forward as evidence for ancestral ties (Emeneau 1938; Hockings 1997). Thus there is no strong evidence for a migration, and also too much reliance on folklore and the rough observations of Ferreira and British colonial officials, even though it has been taken for granted by previous writers.

For these reasons, I disagree with assertions that Badaga legends are 'prime evidence' (p. 5), 'highly credible' (p. 3), and 'there is no doubt that before they settled in the Nilgiris the homeland of the Badagas lay in the Mysore Plain' (Hockings 1980a, p. 11). Similarly, Heidemann's (2014, p. 94) comment that 'there is no doubt that the origin of the Badagas is in the Kannada-speaking region north of the Nilgiri' is also doubtful. Unfortunately, Badagas have been misrepresented in the literature with a migrant identity (and even if Badagas today do have migrant ancestors, their presence in the Nilgiri Hills for several centuries means the migrant character bestowed on them is unhelpful). Dialectology currently being pursued by Christiane Pilot-Raichoor could lead to alternative propositions regarding the history of Badagas, as her findings of grammatical homogeneity of Badagu and the languages of Kotas,

Kurumbas, and Todas might indicate they have always resided in the Nilgiri Hills (Thiagarajan 2012). Also, genetic studies show Badagas share similarities with other indigenous people in the Nilgiris, for example a high incidence of Sickle Cell Trait and HLA antigen distribution, although research is limited to the African origin of humans (Lehmann and Cutbrush 1952; Vishwanathan et al. 2003). In summary, then, separation of Badagas from other people based on history and migration seems unfounded.

Localisation in the Nilgiri Hills

Ideas about location and region figure prominently in writings, and characterise Badagas with certain traits. Based on the tradition in anthropology of spatially local-ized cultures as objects of study, the Nilgiri Hills is typically characterised as a cultural enclave of more than a dozen hill tribes which until recently were isolated from lower plains by a harsh environment. The image in the literature of a remote island shielded by dangerous animals (snakes, tigers and leopards), deadly diseases (malaria), Kurumba sorcerers, steep escapements, and thick blankets of subtropical forest, which supposedly permitted only brief and sporadic contact with the outside world (Ferreira 1603; Hockings 1999; King 1870; Whitehouse 1873; Rivers 1906; Walker 1986), comes across as something out of a Tarzan or Indiana Jones film! The hills versus plains narrative, an extreme contrast of highlands and lowlands, portrays the antiquity, peculiarity, and geographical separation of an island-like location, and disconnection of its population and their cultures from those who bordered it. Other aspects of the Nilgiri Hills have also been regarded as distinctive within South India, such as its climate and 'environmental peculiarity and individuality' (von Lengerke and Blasco, 1989, p. 62). Singling out the Nilgiri Hills along these lines dates to the expedition of Ferreira (1603) who is described as venturing to far away mountains in search of uncontacted Christian communities established at the time of the mar-tyrdom of St. Thomas at Mylapor (Whitehouse 1873; Rivers 1906), and continued in the writings of British colonial officials and visitors. Academic writers also imag-ined a distinct and special area developing on the periphery of mainstream society, unmoved by South Indian culture, and not integrated with the State, markedly dif-ferent to South India and the general population (Mandelbaum 1989; Walker 1989). These perspectives were reinforced by conventional ethnography which concerned single sites understood as bounded islands and cultures with local social relations. This is clearly seen, for example, in the title of works such as *Blue Mountains: The Ethnography and Biogeography of a South Indian Region.*

People in the Nilgiri Hills have also been spatially separated from each other in writings. Colonists and early anthropologists with Euro-American styles of thinking mapped people into neat and tidy spatially-bound entities based on putatively common characteristics, thereby producing rigid identities and boundaries (Mahias 1997). Although any village of one group was within a short walk of the others (Mandelbaum 1941), they have been described as claiming distinct spatial territo-

ries: Todas lived on the western side of the Nilgiri Plateau at elevations ranging
2000–2400 m; Badagas mainly inhabited the eastern half at elevations ranging
2200–1200 m; Kotas were interspersed among Badagas; and Kurumbas lived mainly
on the steep slopes at elevations ranging 1600–600 m (Bird-David 1997; Hockings
1980a; Walker 1986). The different zones are shown diagrammatically in Hockings
(1989, p. 366). A similar artefact is the spatial separation of the Nilgiri Plateau—the
top of the mountain range and its Badagas, Kotas, and Todas—and the Nilgiri-
Wynaad on the lower western slopes a dozen kilometres down with its groups of
Badagas, Chettis, Kotas, Kurumbas, Nayakas, Paniyas, and Todas. Bird-David (1997,
p. 6) even regards them as 'two regional social worlds' with significant differences,
although almost all studies of Badagas concern the plateau and disregard the Wynaad.

Thus the literature implies the existence of an objectively apparent Badaga community with clear-cut boundaries and constituent parts working together to promote
solidarity and stability, namely customs, norms, and institutions with specific functions working in tandem. The notion of a close-knit, spatially-bounded, and isolated
community implies similarity and difference, a relational idea of one community in
contrast to another, but in reality it is an ideological notion based on how it appears to
academics looking in from an external and biased vantage point. A recent estimation
(Hockings 2013) put the community at more than 160,000 people and 390 hamlets.
However, the exact size is unknown as they have not been enumerated as a separate
group in the Census of India since 1981. It is difficult to think of people in the Nilgiri
Hills as spatially bounded and isolated communities. Although mobility might seem
truer today than ever before, people in times past was also mobile and connected.
Globalization is not necessarily a new phenomenon but a historical process which has
occurred since ancient times. The authorities in the colonial period often portrayed
the Indian population as fixed and immobile, and much of the literature on the Nilgiris follows this trend with false assumptions of sedentary patterns as the norm, and
population movement as an exclusively modern phenomenon. Yet historical research
shows that most of the Indian rural population was highly mobile at that time, and
population movement was the rule rather than exception.

A minority of writers have touched on similarities and linkages between Badagas
and the wider South Indian context. These include, for example, fluency in Dravidian
languages, kinship systems, Shaivism, emphasis on pollution and purity, and gift
exchange in previous times (Mandelbaum 1989; Rivers 1906; Walker 1989; Zagarell
1997). Rivers (1906) commented that the assumed differences in customs and
ceremonies between people in the Nilgiris and elsewhere in India could be slighter
than initially thought. Mandelbaum (1989) also revised his perspective as he came to
know India better. An underlying theme of Walker's recent update of Todas was consideration of the people within the Hindu world of South India (Walker 1986, 1989).
Although more research is needed, there is preliminary evidence of extensive and
long-term relationships among people in the Nilgiri Hills and bordering areas and
their integration into the mainstream in ancient times. For example, archaeological
research shows prehistoric cultures in the area did not develop in a vacuum (Zagarell
1997), despite earlier excavation reports (Breeks 1873; Hockings 1975; Naik 1966)
which claimed its monuments diverged from the types typifying much of South

India during the megalithic period. Other linkages mentioned in passing in previous writings include trading expeditions in Tamil Nadu by Badagas, petty trading of merchandise in the Nilgiris by Chettis, a group styled as merchants (Ferreira 1603; Francis 1908; Zagarell 1997), and immigration throughout the centuries. Another point to consider here is the supposed migration of the ancestors of Badagas several hundred years ago, and the subsequent founding of the Badaga community in the Nilgiri Hills, a key theme in folklore and academic literature. If the migration had really happened, then Badagas might have retained connections and some aspects of their residual identities, although they would have lost many connections; indeed, they lost their alleged former caste identity as Vokkaliga. It is ironic these linkages and similarities were not explored in detail by previous writers as they would have challenged the prevailing stereotype of isolation and difference.

Badagas as One Big Family

Another misrepresentation in the literature is the organization of an apparent Badaga population around family ties, descent groups, and kinship. The Dravidian kinship system has typically been used to identify relatedness, marriage arrangements, land ownership transfer, and responsibility for life-cycle rituals. The Badaga community has been subdivided into the following kinship groups in order of magnitude: extended families of several generations in the same home or neighbouring houses, minimal or minor lineages in a village, major lineages in neighboring villages, maximal lineages, forty-four clans, and ten phratries or subcastes (Hockings 1980a, 1999). A key difference between these kinship groups was exogamy, whereby marriage was permitted only with a partner outside the group, or endogamy; generally, but not always, Badagas practiced exogamy up to the phratry level, and their community was endogamous. Badagas have also been characterized with the Dakota-Iroquois (bifurcate merging) kinship nomenclature which distinguishes between generations, maternal and paternal sides of family, and siblings of opposite sexes in the parental generation. The distinction determined eligibility of marriage partner based on preferential patterns of bilateral cross-cousin marriage, which is typical of Dravidian kinship systems generally, and the characterization of property inheritance as being passed down the male lineage (Hockings 1999). Kinship also underpinned the panchayat system (Grigg 1880; Mantramurti 1981; Thurston and Rangachari 1909). The Badaga community has been described as a chiefdom, a social hierarchy of authority monopolized by headmen (senior members of select families determined by birth and nearness by kinship, as headmanships descended patrilineally within families). Each village, commune, and division of the Nilgiri Hills was headed by a respected and influential male elder aided by a small council of male elders (Hockings 1980a; Mantramurti 1981; Thurston and Rangachari 1909). They played a vital role in the general life of villages and community by settling disputes, and offering advice on important issues, as detailed by Hockings (1980a) and Mantramurti (1981). Heidemann (2014) notes there are now two types of Badaga leaders:

'Traditional leaders' in villages presiding over councils, and 'modern leaders' who belong to political parties in India and deal with local and state governments.

Formal kinship analysis in the traditions of Morgan, Levi-Strauss, and Radcliffe-Brown was in fashion at the time the research was conducted in the Nilgiris, and therefore writings followed a trend of kinship terminologies, marriage rules, and customary authority which tied a reified Badaga identity to hereditary criteria while neglecting kinship practice in daily life. An unfortunate consequence is emphasis on the togetherness of Badagas, a distinctively relational mode of identification which implies genetic relatedness and family ties, and descent from a common ancestor, and the distinctiveness and exclusivity of the group as different from its neighbours reinforced by ideas of same-caste marriage (endogamy of caste), and prohibition of intimate relations and (intercaste) marriage with other groups. This portrayal of Badagas emphasised one large family united by the past (evolutionary origin, genetics, and shared descent) and the future (descendants not yet born, and kinship rules such as inheritance patterns), even though the group is too large to maintain a sense of shared kinship, and not everyone is interested in or has access to information about common origins, descent and other criteria included in such academic constructions of identity (Chapter "Badagas Going Digital" also reveals young people are confused by traditional marriage rules based on kinship terminologies). These writings about principles of descent are based on old styles of thinking about primitive societies when blood, descent, and territoriality were assumed to equate with race and ethnicity, based on assumptions that group membership is fixed, and complementary with other unifying criteria proposed in the literature, namely culture and language. Also, even though Badagas and other South Indians had the same sort of descent system, which basically consisted of anthropological ideas of patrilineal and segmented lineage systems with ultimogeniture, the literature on the Nilgiris tends to separate rather than unite them. Some of the writings by adventurers and missionaries even mention ideas of genetically transmitted physical differences between people in the Nilgiri Hills (e.g. phrenology; Marshall 1873), another tendency to think of social categories as biologically distinctive populations. Yet in earlier periods of human history, people and groups intermingled, which means objective identification of ethnicity based on genetics and hereditary is generally unworkable. Singling out Badagas as genetically different is also wrong because the category is a cultural and social phenomenon shaped by various social forces—e.g. artificially bounding the Nilgiri Hills, arbitrarily designating distinct points in time (e.g. migration), and the naming and labeling of people under colonial rule—and not biological. The idea that there is somehow a distinctive type of Badaga DNA is fiction. While genetics research is needed, a substantial genetic proximity of a Badaga population seems very unlikely as it is a cultural group, and not based on biology or genetic purity, and has never been static. Another bias is the remarkable similarity between accounts of the panchayat system (e.g. Hockings 1980a, p. 171) and the modern legal system, and labelling of headmen with colonial terms such as 'Paramount Chief'. A more fruitful line of enquiry would be to use kinship to debate Badaga identities, as writings do not incorporate the theoretical theme of identities with ethnographic derived notions of kinship, unlike recent approaches that have since been published on other cultural groups.

Language, Religion, and Folk Medicine

Badagas and other indigenous people in the Nilgiri Hills are thought to have mutually unintelligible Dravidian languages, although only a few have been studied (Emeneau 1989). Badagu, also known as Badaga, is spoken only by Badagas, although the majority of people are bilingual or trilingual, typically fluent in Badagu, English, and Tamil. Badagu is not a written language, and oral tradition takes the form of ballads, curses, folktales, legends, omens, plays, poetry, prayers, proverbs, sayings, and songs. Compilations and translations of Badagu have been published (Hockings and Pilot-Raichoor 1992). Some Badagas are accomplished singers, and have released albums in Badagu and Tamil for sale and distribution. However, research is sparse, especially when contrasted to Kota and Toda languages (Emeneau 1944–1946; Mandelbaum 1941).

The origin and classification of Badagu has been debated, and Hockings (1980a) suggests there are six dialects. One proposition is that Badagu is a dialect or variant form of Old Kannada retained from migrant ancestors from the former Mysore, mixed with recent innovation as well as some assimilation of Nilgiri languages, and therefore now a closely related yet separate language (Agesthialingom 1972; Emeneau 1939, 1967). Since 1981, Badagu has been categorized in the Census of India in the 'Kannada, Badaga and Kodagu' sub-group of the Dravidian family which lumps together Badagu and Kannada speakers, which can perhaps be taken to mean that Badagu is officially regarded as a dialect of Kannada. An alternative perspective put forward by Pilot-Raichoor is that Badagu is typologically very different to Kannada, based on comparisons of phonology, morphology, syntax, and lexicon; for example, Badagu contains many words of English, Persian, Tamil, and Sanskrit origin, and its core grammar converges with other Nilgiri languages, indicative perhaps of a separate language rather than a Kannada dialect (Hockings and Pilot-Raichoor 1992; Thiagarajan 2012).

Another criterion of distinctiveness in previous studies is religion. The majority of Badagas are followers of Shaivism, a popular sect of Hinduism, and nearly every village has a temple devoted to Shiva. Although the Shaivism they practice is typical of most Hindus in South India, it is claimed their 'village Hinduism' has unique features including worship of minor deities, e.g. folk heroes regarded as founders of their community in the Nilgiri Hills (Metz 1864). One example is the Goddess Hette, the mythical founder of several villages, typically portrayed in folklore as the ideal women and the guardian of health and agriculture (Belli Gowder 1923–1941; Benbow 1930; Breeks 1873; Grigg 1880; Harkness 1832; Hockings 1989, 1999; Metz 1864; Thurston and Rangachari 1909). She is worshipped in an annual festival by thousands of devotees. A smaller proportion of Badagas (over 10,000) are adherents of Lingayatism. Several thousand people also follow Christianity since previous generations in the mid-nineteenth century succumbed to Protestant and Roman Catholic missionary activities (although only a small proportion converted). The first missionary stations established in the Nilgiri Hills were in 1846 and 1867 by the Basel Mission, a Christian missionary society of different Protestant denominations.

Hockings (1980b) published a medical ethnography of folk medicine among Badagas which implied a distinct approach to health and illness. Only 49 of more than 120 species of medicinal herbs he identified in a village were mentioned in books of Ayurvedic and Sidda medicine, and they had different usage. It has also been reported that Badagas performed distinct health-related life-cycle rituals for pregnancy, birth, childhood, old-age, and death (Hockings 1980b; Thurston and Rangachari 1909). Each indigenous group including Badagas has been described as having their own distinct folk medicine, but I cannot find any empirical evidence to support the claim. Although Hockings reported the existence of Badaga folk medicine, his research was based on only one village (Oranayi), and therefore not generalizable. Also, the research was done in the 1960s when only a handful of elderly therapists remained in the community. My enquiries in the Nilgiris suggest the folk medicine is now extinct or never existed. Moreover, Hockings believed the therapists practiced idiosyncratic folk therapies rather than a common medical system, for the following reasons: Virilocal residence meant health beliefs were localised and passed down by oral tradition, as there were no medical texts or schools; therapists were secretive as they believed the efficacy of herbal remedies diminished when disclosed; and each therapist worked creatively. Indeed, it seems logical that local variations in folk medicine would have existed throughout the Nilgiris, especially prior to biomedicine introduced by missionaries and government hospitals established in the 1830s, but whether they constitute distinct types of folk medicine is debatable.

Traditional Economy

Another example of identity construction in the literature is gift exchange and reciprocity among people in the Nilgiri Hills. As the well known story goes, Badagas and other people prior to the mid-nineteenth century interdepended on economic and ritual exchanges of products and services. It is claimed relationships performed the function of disposing surplus grain produce, and, for the vast majority of people, satisfied their basic requirements of food, goods, and services. Although first documented by Ferreira (1603) and nineteenth century writers (Breeks 1873; Harkness 1832; Metz 1864), Rivers (1906) published a detailed analysis which was later updated and refined by Mandelbaum (1941). It has since been extensively discussed and popularized, and is one reason the Nilgiris is well known. The early writings centred on Badagas, Kotas, Kurumbas and Todas in the 'Nilgiri Plateau'. Recent work reported other groups such as Chettis, Kadu Nayakas, Kurumbas and Paniyas (Misra 1972); and Badagas, Kotas and Todas in the Wynaad, a lower area to the northwest (Bird-David 1997). Although each ethnic group was able to satisfy most of their needs by their own efforts, and had multiple and overlapping economic and social practices, the literature accentuates the uniqueness and distinctiveness of their roles with generalisations, stereotypes, and duties which have been uncritically repeated in many writings: Badagas have been portrayed as agriculturalists; Kotas as the artisans, blacksmiths, builders, carpenters, leather-workers, and potters of the Nilgiris; Todas, numbering barely a few hundred, have been characterised as pastoralists, and their culture as being centered on their herds of buffalos which they ritualized through animal care and dairy practices; and Kurumbas as food gatherers, hunters, swidden cultivators, and sorcerers (Breeks 1873; Harkness 1832; Metz 1864; Thurston and Rangachari 1909; Ward 1821). Apparently, Badagas were the main agriculturalists, and the only group which produced a real surplus of grain, as the other groups grew barely enough for their own needs. They traded grain at harvest time along with other items in return for various products and services, as they had no specialized craftsmen (Hockings 1980a; Metz 1864; Thurston and Rangachari 1909).

Scholars have debated whether gift exchange in the Nilgiri Hills was an early prototype of the Indian caste system (Gould 1967; Hockings 1980a; Mandelbaum 1941; Walker 1986). Mandelbaum (1956, 1989) likened it to the classic jatis or jajmani caste system which prevailed over rural India in the nineteenth century. Both were characterised as separate, interdependent social groups in a locality each with provision of goods and services and occupational specializations and unique customs, and cooperative activities between families, with some characteristics of a contract alongside wider and warmer relationships. That the Nilgiri people interacted in a generally friendly and peaceful social system has prompted some authors (Fry et al. 2008) to repackage it as a 'peace system' of neighbouring non-warring societies underpinned by moral and social values and harmonious social relationships, and certain psychosocial features which prevented warfare and promoted a culture of peace. Strong incentives against waging war in the Nilgiri Hills included social relationships, which were valued and based on trust, as trade was not reciprocated for several months or more; hereditary trading relationships passed from father to son (indeed, many of the relationships are thought to have been passed down generations between lineages in the respective communities through patrilineally descending partnerships); and no militia or weapons of war (Fry et al. 2008). However, arguments can also be made against the notion of a peace system including cases of hostilities and tensions ranging from stigmatisation (for example, Kurumbas were stereotyped negatively as primitive hunter-gatherers, sellers of forest produce, and mystics) to violent retributions such as witchcraft murders of Kurumbas and Todas.

The writings on gift exchange had important implications for the ways Badagas have been portrayed. The gifts and roles can be interpreted as group identities concentrated on functional aspects and mechanics of gift exchange. The stereotypes created, defined, and isolated each group and their relations with ascribed behaviour with associates which dramatised group boundaries and social status, even though they did not exclusively pursue the activities in the stereotypes, and descriptions of the groups seem contradictory. For example, the sorcery of Badagas was contrasted to that of Kurumbas and Todas; all groups engaged in subsistence agriculture and hunting even though it is often claimed otherwise; and others were involved in trade of goods and ritual services even though it was often depicted simply as four or so groups. Similar to other functionalist descriptions of people in the Nilgiri Hills, it was also described as a system or institution with customs that established social order among different ethnic groups linked together, based on uncritical acceptance by previous writers of generalizations which seem to exaggerate differences between groups. Gift exchange in the Nilgiri Hills might be an artefact in reports of the colonial administration which ascribed certain characteristics and mannerisms to members of groups that made them suitable for certain occupations, to meet the exigencies of daily rule, although my suggestion requires further consideration.

Badagas as Colonial Subjects

The rule of the British Crown in the Indian subcontinent is a reoccurring theme in the literature on the Nilgiris, and is typically depicted as a seismic event in terms of social transformation. It is claimed that changes began with the acquisition of the region in 1799 by The East India Company under the Madras Presidency, as part of lands annexed from the territory of Tipu Sultan. There was a tendency to categorise the history of the Nilgiri Hills into three principal periods—aboriginal, colonial, and Independence (Mandelbaum 1989)—which put colonial rule at centre stage in social change, as if the area suddenly come into existence when the British arrived.

John Sullivan, Collector of Coimbatore between 1815 and 1830, is usually associated with the beginnings of the principal towns Ootacamund and Coonoor, and the seasonal shift of the capital of Madras Presidency to Ootacamund. The principal hill stations became renowned in colonial British society as an enclave of British culture as well as a refuge from the summer heat (Kennedy 1996; Mandelbaum 1989). Europeans and South Indians relocated to the area, and comprised a sizeable proportion of the population (Heidemann 1997). Development of the area included buildings, factories, railways, roads, missionary stations, and a military base, embedded in social reforms, commercialization of agriculture, infrastructure and transport construction, demarcation of sovereignty, land taxes, and population surveillance.

It has been suggested that Badagas remained relatively unchanged until these encounters with European and South Indian cultures which significantly impacted on their way of life (Mandelbaum 1941). This can be illustrated, for example, with accounts of agricultural development. Prior to the creation of a cash economy, people practised subsistence agriculture, initially slash-and-burn farming (Grigg 1880). Commercial-style plantations were established in the 1830s, and animal husbandry declined due to conversion of grazing land to plantations. By the 1850s, agricultural practices focused on cash crops (cabbage, potato) and animal products for sale in markets rather than local consumption. Another example of change was the demise of gift and commodity relationships in the Nilgiri Hills which are thought to have remained the same until the 1930s (Emeneau 1938; Hockings 1980a). Although the reasons are actually speculative, writings emphasise the role of the economic reforms in British India. As the new cash economy apportioned market value to products and services, the price of grain that Badagas donated to others was apparently higher than the prices of goods they received, which meant it became logical to buy products in markets to satisfy their needs more cheaply (and also conveniently, as the old relations were relatively time-consuming; Mandelbaum 1955). It is also thought the relations with the increasing number of migrants replaced the former exchanges (Mandelbaum 1989; Heidemann 1997).

Hockings (1989) believes the changes in British India were concentrated in the towns, and initially had minimal influence on Badagas. However, they gradually came in contact with the new orientations towards life. It has been suggested they were the first ethnic minority in the Nilgiri Hills to change—for example, to intensive cash-crop cultivation, employment in local businesses, education of children in missionary schools, and the establishment of authority by British officials which undermined the panchayat headmen—whereas the other groups maintained their traditional way of life for several more decades (Mandelbaum 1941, 1989; Hockings 1999). Reasons hypothesised for their readiness to change include their history of migration which meant they had common ground for interaction, and closer proximity to the new way of life (Mandelbaum 1941, 1989; Hockings 1999). Mandelbaum wrote the British carried certain legitimacy as they were regarded as the Kshatriya Varna, the social division of a Hindu society synonymous with the ruling elite; he also reasoned that Badagas readily adopted the ways of Tamils and Kannadas as they 'took the modernising Hindus when they met as models of change' (Mandelbaum 1989, p. 15).

The colonial era was important for documenting quality of life among Badagas. East India Company officers initiated social research in the Nilgiris by collecting information on agriculture, customs, economy, population, and trade. Census data were first compiled in 1812. District Gazetteers (comprehensive catalogues of data) were compiled by officials, first in Madras in 1853, and then in other districts in the late 19th Century onwards (Francis 1908; Grigg 1880; Ouchterlony 1868; Ward 1821). The chapters on the Nilgiris describe its administration, agriculture, communication networks, education provision, forests, land revenue, local government, occupations, people, political history, public health, and trade. Hockings (1999) reported improvements in their life quality in colonial India including commercial farming, increased life expectancy, access to school education, and the emergence of an urbanised middle class. However, previous writings are concerned with imperial history and Western culture to speak for Badagas. Studies of the Nilgiri Hills began when anthropology was emerging as an academic discipline and derived many of its key notions from colonialism. Recent work seems less prone to gross ethnocentrism, but still comes across on occasions as a nostalgic and idyllic return to the colonial past. An example of this bias is the use of concepts such as 'development', 'modern' and 'success' to portray the colonial period and its influence on the quality of life of Badagas in positive terms. Mandelbaum, for example, believed Badagas 'flourished', 'took advantage of' (1982, p. 1460), and 'benefited from' (1989, p. 15) the changes. Hockings (1999) even concluded Badagas in the 1990s represented a 'successful' South Indian community because they had evolved markedly over several centuries from several hundred refugees to a 'powerful' and 'wealthy' community in South India, which he attributed to their 'progressive attitudes' to accepting British customs (1999, p. 18). British civil servants have even been labelled as 'revolutionary', and their actions as a 'cultural revolution' (Hockings 1989, p. 334). As Hockings (1997, p. 3) wrote, "The Nilgiris…had been an isolated backwater vis-à-vis the militaristic neighbouring states in the plains until in 1820 the British founded Ootacamund and began to settle in the hills". These derogatory expressions, reminiscent of the cultural, economic, and political aspirations of the West, position a new way of life in the Nilgiri Hills in British India as superior to the past, as authors tend to take the position that Badaga culture and lifestyles should be replaced with British ones, and write as if colonialism and its large-scale cultural diffusion is what past and present is all about.

Thus academic discourse locates Badagas as colonial subjects who assume an identity ascribed by the colonizer and the Nilgiris as a product of colonialism, a legitimating narrative of cultural domination. It mirrors old-fashioned views when social scientists believed minority groups adopted the culture of the majority (cultural assimilation), as adjustments among Badagas have been interpreted as a one-way imperialistic process of assimilation or integration within a mainstream society, and two forms of bounded undifferentiated cultures coming into contact—the 'Badagas' and 'British'. The British were assumed to be the normal and desirable majority culture and Badagas the eccentric minority, as if cultural change functions to celebrate a privileged access to a hegemonic British culture. The displacement of Badagas and other Indian people during colonialism in favour of the politically dominant group lays claim to epistemological privilege, a racialised agenda which reveals more about historical relationships of knowledge and power than it does about Badagas. For example, there has been no consideration of the responses of the British and their incorporation of cultural products from people in the Nilgiris, which implies the latter has nothing of importance to contribute to cultural innovation. I also take issue with previous writers' interpretations of 'tradition', 'modern' and 'success'. Who is to say what the standards for success might be for Badagas? Previous writers espoused the conventional thinking of their day when modernisation emphasised an evolutionary trajectory of progress from so-called traditional (underdeveloped) societies, a short-hand way of referring to agrarian societies before the impact of the recent West, to modern (industrial) societies, quality of life after the impact of the West in economic, political, social, and technological terms. Discourses on modernity in India were initially concerned with application of these European theories and models, and the writings on the Nilgiris fit in with this trend. However, recent studies on India have interrogated the various perspectives of modernity, which do not lend to such easy definition. Indeed, modernity is now a highly contested topic, and recent theorists have challenged classical models with India-specific orientations, giving rise to alternative claims and a rethink of classical discourse, although these developments have been ignored in the literature on the Nilgiris. It is also surprising that Indian post-colonial identities have been overlooked in Nilgiri studies but feature prominently in writings about the post-independence nation-building effort in India.

Misra (1999) reminds us that quality of life is not only about academic musing but real people. 'The British took away the land of the ancient inhabitants and imposed taxes on them making the local inhabitants realize where the power was. For themselves they created conditions of luxury and pleasure in home-like conditions…The non-white inhabitants of the Nilgiris worked hard under the most oppressive conditions to run the colonial-plantation structure. The Whites over the years had become accustomed to luxury as they were carried on rickshaws from the plains of Coimbatore region to the heights of the Nilgiris pulled up by local inhabitants, most of them the Badagas'. Misra also argued these conditions were attractive to Western ethnographers, and enabled them to conduct their studies in comfort while the local way of life and social and natural environment were completely and irreversibly replaced with a capitalist one characterized by money, domination, and social inequality. Moreover, the policies of the British Raj were exploitative, as the region was ruled with considerable power by relatively small numbers of British (Misra 1999). The opening of the Western Ghats for plantations involved land grabs and relocations, and plantations in colonial India are well known for cruel working conditions and hardships which were integral to nationalist struggles. Negative aspects of colonialism in the Nilgiris and India have been glossed over in earlier writings on Badagas to portray some kind of path to utopia, although it is also important not to overlook the positive aspects of colonialism such as agricultural methods, hospitals, schools, and other services, a major improvement in quality of life.

Even if these portrayals of a successful Badaga community in the Nilgiri Hills and its underlying causes are taken at face value, they still seem difficult to accept in light of hardships people have suffered since the 1990s. Tea cultivation comprises the mainstay of their rural economy (a survey undertaken in 2001 indicated 86% of Nilgiri smallholders grew only tea; Neilson and Pritchard 2009). The livelihoods of farmers hinge on prices of cash crops in national and global markets which have been susceptible to significant variations. Although high tea prices in the mid-1990s supported high returns and rising affluence, prices dropped sharply in the late 1990s onwards when India's share of the export market declined due to quality issues and rising competition from new tea-producing countries. Badagas were affected by these issues, and suffered economic hardship. Also, they generally have small production quantities constrained by small plots of land and limited capital, skills, supplies, and market information. They compete with large tea estates and companies equipped with vast resources. Although the early twentieth century saw the emergence of wealthy Badagas and owners of plantations (Ranga 1934), the majority were smallholders or landless labourers working on plantations (Grigg 1880). Neilson and Pritchard (2009) provide a timely summary of the 'tea crisis' in the Nilgiris and its impact on the quality of life. They estimated the annual income of Badaga smallholders decreased 82% between 1998 and 2001, as average green leaf prices decreased 50% from Rs. 12/kg to Rs. 5.95/kg. To make up for lost income, smallholders took shortcuts in felling, pruning, and pest and disease management, with consequences for the quality of tea they produced. Some families abandoned agriculture, sold their land, and left the Nilgiris. In 2001, 60,389 tea smallholders were enumerated in the Nilgiris, but in 2006 the number had fallen to 50,329 (Neilson and Pritchard 2009). So do Badagas really represent a successful South Indian community, as portrayed in the literature? Although the switch to cash-crop cultivation improved living standards, and some people enjoy a high standard of living, the majority have faced quality of life challenges.

Desire for Change

Badagas have taken action to improve their living conditions and the ways they are portrayed by others. An example is a large rally on May 15th 1989 which included a procession to the District Collector's Office in Ootacamund, and submission of a memorandum addressed to the Chief Minister of Tamil Nadu with demands for minimum prices of agricultural products and recognition as a Scheduled Tribe (Heidemann 2014). Since the 1990s, the date of the rally has been designated 'Badaga Day' to commemorate and celebrate their culture, history, and political unity with activities: communal meals, dance, gatherings, prayers to goddess Hette, public speeches, processions, and worship of the bust of H. B. Ari Gowder (Heidemann 2014). Many other protests have taken place over the years including demands, delegation visits to government departments and the Tea Board, and small- and large-scale gatherings. According to Heidemann (2014), the events unite the community as a whole with feelings of oneness and self-representation, and mark their presence and visibility as a distinct group to a large audience locally and further afield. 'This cultural display identifies groups, highlights cultural markers, and underlines political claims. Culture is externalized and becomes a thing that can be sensed' (Heidemann 2014, p. 92). Heidemann contends the central feature of the 1989 rally was oneness, as many Badagas congregated as a homogenous whole in one large space in close proximity with coordinated behaviour, a symbol of cultural autonomy, harmony, and solidarity.

Heidemann (2014) puts emphasis on the presence of the State in self-representations as Badaga at the rally in 1989. The memorandum was handed over in a meeting between leaders of the Badaga community and the state government, and it contained objectified descriptions of Badaga culture which were incorporated into government files, a hybrid of traditional and modern aspects of life. Similarly, he interprets Badaga Day to be a celebration of both the cultural self and the State, as government representatives are welcomed and honoured at events which emphasise traditional aspects of Badaga culture. Another example of hybridity according to Heidemann is Badagas working as public servants and government employees, thereby representing both Badagas and the Government in a single form and place. In other words, Badagas constitute a distinct group with their own culture and community, but at the same time are integrated into the State. An inherent contradiction in his reasoning, however, is reification of two forms of bounded cultures coming into contact based on assumptions of distinctiveness as separate entities, which overlooks performative notions of identities, creolization and fusion, and post-structuralist cultural theory. Unfortunately, such perspectives have not been explored by previous writers.

To strengthen their case for becoming a Scheduled Tribe, the content of memorandums written by Badagas have extensive quotations from 19th century anthropologist-administrators, and emphasise criteria reminiscent of animist or totemic religions, distinctive culture, economic backwardness, geographical isolation, lack of relationship to the majority, and 'primitive' traits. Some Badagas believe they are clearly separated from other minorities in the Nilgiris, and deserving of distinctive rights. However, as this chapter shows, these claims are inaccurate and fail to recognise these markers as constructions of colonists and scholars. Badagas are not different to, and no more indigenous than, other South Indians, and so the memorandum was based on false premises. Also, it seems contradictory that some Badagas at the events concurrently construct both positive and negative images of their caste, the former based on feelings of pride and togetherness, and the latter on disadvantage and unfairness, in claims for a new identity to claim government entitlements, privilege, and recognition. Therefore, their demands for improvements in quality of life can be interpreted as grapples with self, ultimately questioning the value of being Badaga.

Cultural autonomy as Badaga has also been constructed as a political identity with important implications for quality of life. Badagas are pigeonholed by the Indian government as a Backward Class, one of several official classifications along with Scheduled Caste (Untouchables) and Scheduled Tribe (aboriginal or Adivasi or tribal), in contrast to the general castes. Badagas claim their elders in the 1950s rejected the Government's proposal of classification as a Scheduled Tribe as it was perceived to be demeaning at the time. However, some have since campaigned for the title to secure government assistance including greater proportion of quotas for jobs in central and state governments, and reserved seats in educational institutions, parliament, and provincial legislative assemblies. The rally in 1989 and other events can be regarded as strategies to achieve this goal, and therefore to advance within the political system based on distributive justice. It is political because if their demands are met, the group's political strength in terms of its representation and power to influence the Government to claim preferential entitlements and resources to improve quality of life would be asserted. Importantly, identity politics shows the Badaga category revolves around highly contested notions of identities. For example, if Badagas become lumped together with other Scheduled Tribes in the Nilgiri Hills, new demarcations between them and other South Indians will be created, whereas the current grouping of Badagas and the Hindu majority would be severed. Furthermore, Scheduled Tribes are generally stereotyped in India as backward, and geographically concentrated in the hilly and forested terrain of the plateau regions of India (even though the populations grouped under the category are extremely diverse), which has implications for how Badagas would be perceived in the future (while 'Scheduled Tribe' may at first appear relatively unproblematic, it is actually highly ambiguous and contestable, and there has been no real debate or consensus over its implications for Badagas). Yet Badagas are not alone in their endeavour. Since the creation of the Scheduled Tribe category in the 1950s, the number of groups listed has increased. They can also be situated in issues surrounding indigenist advocacy and politics constructed at global and local levels. As in other cases, indigeneity as an identity has become a powerful tool that Badagas deploy for self-affirmation and political mobilization to influence the distribution of resources and power. It should also be noted that calls by Badagas for the Scheduled Tribe identity have been continuing for decades. Like a vinyl record, the issue is continually going around and around in the same groove and getting nowhere. Also, as shown in Chapter "Badagas Going Digital", not every Badaga desires to be a Scheduled Tribe, as there is a diversity of opinions and claims and counterclaims. Therefore, demands for becoming a Scheduled Tribe likely represent a site of contestation rather than the oneness portrayed in the literature, and requires further delineation.

Concluding Summary and Chapter Outlines

To set the scene, this introductory chapter is a review of different representations of Badagas in previous writings, and the cultural, historical, and political processes which have shaped the construction of a distinct cultural and ethnic identity category representing a specific population and way of life. It offers an overview of the key social actors and contexts and their epistemological claims involved in the creation of the category, and has relevance to depictions of other ethnic minority people in India. There seems to be a universal agreement in the literature that Badagas are a distinct social group sharing a common history and culture framed by markers of similarity and solidarity. Criteria and group boundaries reviewed above include caste, community, gift exchange, folk medicine, history, kinship, language, locality, political mobilisation, and religion, which have been especially important in shaping a reified identity. Although previous writings meticulously document their culture and quality of life, they are simplified and misleading. Penned in a language and mind-set characteristic of colonists and early anthropologists, and within the convention of evolutionary theory and primitive society, European explorers imagined themselves as different and superior to an exotic and peculiar group of people, an artefact of othering processes. Unfortunately, these styles of depiction continued in the first and latter halves of the twentieth century as scholars continued to report in greater detail the various artefacts of an assumed Badaga character. While later work signalled an improvement, Badagas continue to be imagined as a distinct and primitive microcosm isolated from the South Indian majority, a spatially-bounded, close-knit, and structured system or community with unique constituent parts (customs, norms, and institutions) working in unity and stability, and writings come across as if the scholar's role is auxiliary to a British explorer or colonial administrator. The literature, for the most part written by white men visiting a far-away place, and who took dark-skinned 'savages' as their specialty, emphasised the characteristics of a long-lost ancient human society; for example, descriptions of exotic customs such as exorcism, sacrifice of goats and sheep, and fire-walking activities (Hockings 1980a). Assumptions about antiquity and primitiveness in the nineteenth century spawned debate about evolutionism, as the cultures in the Nilgiri Hills were regarded as ancient and prototypical of the original type or model of South Indian culture. Anthropologists at that time were searching for autochthonous, unknown races, and early emphasis on the Nilgiris was partly to engage evolutionary theory.

A functionalist stance is particularly noticeable in previous writings which give people a limited sense of agency, written about as if they are puppets acting as their role requires, relatively fixed and concrete notions of reality devoid of shared subjective experiences and meanings in daily life. Regarding quality of life, for example, the majority of writings are concerned with imperial history and Western culture, and emphasise the new way of life in the Nilgiris after the arrival of the British, and its superiority to the past. Previous research only reported evaluations of economics and living standards (objective quality of life) with no consideration of the views of the people (subjective quality of life), in line with previous academic convention which relegated local people to a passive voice with no agency of their own. Other examples reviewed here include the imputation as rigorously as possible of unique customs or practices and their position and effect in a supposedly cohesive, stable Badaga system: Economic and ritual exchange among groups of people in the Nilgiri Hills; organization of a Badaga society around kinship terminologies and descent groups; rituals portrayed in terms of their social functions and value to society as a whole over the individual; and the practice and assumptions of the classic model of single-site ethnography which regarded Badagas and the Nilgiri Hills as local, bounded, and isolated, and controlled by macro-level factors such as the British Raj and its capitalist political economy. Many of these descriptions are second order theorisations devised and imposed by Western academics rather than Badagas. Even recent updates of the Nilgiris (Hockings 2013; Neilson and Pritchard 2009) still emphasise macro-level constructions of a larger social order: the British Raj and its capitalist political economy, and globalisation and the world economy, broad focus on social structures shaping a primeval human society.

These depictions have persisted as an illusion in the literature, an overemphasis of homogeneity, and downplay of diversity, contradiction, and subjectivities. They raise more questions than answered, largely because the meanings of being Badaga have been taken as so straightforward and unproblematic, a complete absence of grappling with epistemological issues, and there is a noticeable reluctance of accounting for dynamic aspects of identities and people's lives. It is important to reflect on their dangers. The production of discrete groups frame simple stereotypes that accentuate homogeneity within groups and differences rather than similarities between groups (some of which seem insignificant and not worth emphasising), and ignores nuanced meanings and mixed or multiple identities. Unfortunately, the simple researcher-assigned representations have come to be perceived as officially-constituted, even by Badagas themselves, as shown in the memorandum they created in the 1989 rally. The Nilgiri Hills as an isolated cultural enclave of hill tribes is still the prevailing standpoint (Hockings 2013; Neilson and Pritchard 2009), and repeated in recent writings. Although these positions began to wane in the 1960s, and are now effectively dead in social science, surprisingly they are still alive and kicking in the literature on the Nilgiri Hills. Indeed, it is this imagined distinctiveness which has piqued so much interest over the years. My research documented in the following chapters reveals Badagas certainly do not conform to old fashioned styles of Euro-American thinking, and should no longer be characterised simply as a bounded and distinct rural community in the Nilgiri Hills of about 160,000 people with certain proxy measures as cultural and historical traits and a high quality of life. Rather, focus should be on more meaningful and sensitive conceptualisations constructed and produced by the people under study on their judgements of social reality and multiplicity of Badaga life journeys which are much more diverse, complex, and nuanced than previously suggested—and the fact that they are experiencing quality of life difficulties. In other words, this book takes the view there never has been such a thing as a distinctive and reified coherent identity and way of life, and aims to provide fresh thinking and greater flexibility in conceptualisation. The following pages put forward findings which discredit the long-standing reductive depictions of identity and quality of life in the literature as an almost Euro-American invention nested in colonial and academic stances.

The methodology of the research, outlined in the next chapter, is a contemporary social constructionist approach which irons out many of the epistemological problems discussed above. Chapter "Methodology" begins with an overview of its multi-sited standpoint which removes the geographical barriers of previous studies and their relegation of Badagas as local and bounded in an isolated region to appreciate people as dynamic, mobile, and multiply situated, and to capture new forms of identities and quality of life. The next section introduces the theoretical orientation of the research, symbolic interactionism, employed to examine the shared experiences and meanings of Badagas in India with emphasis on agency, social process, and subjectivity, a deliberate move away from previous macro-level deterministic and functionalist thinking. The remaining sections describe the operationalization of quality of life and identity in the research, data collection from Internet forum posts and face-to-face interviews, and data analysis involving coding and thematic analysis. This attention to human self-expression as Badaga permits a more complete understanding which takes into account personal and lived experiences as well as recent work on cosmopolitan, hybrid, and multicultural identities and their intersectionality, in which ideas of rigid criteria and group boundaries have given way to fluidity. The changes taking place in India and among Badagas are considered as a cultural and personal process involving people within local settings and resources, and are not simply about economic and social standards or academic style as often shown in writings.

Based on this methodology, Chapters "Badagas Going Digital" and "Migrants' Voices" empirically investigate the life quality and identities of Badagas in two connected locations, the first online among Internet forum users (city residents), and the second in the real world with rural-to-urban migrants in Bangalore. Specifically, Chapter "Badagas Going Digital" examines online portrayals by Badagas in a virtual community, a website in the form of posted messages. It begins with a note on the paucity of media and visual studies of the Nilgiri Hills and its people, and the role of media as a prime information source and facilitator of cultural change. Next is an analysis of the content of the Internet forum, information about the goings-on of Badagas including their past and current circumstances. As the first study of their new media use, it shows they now have an online presence and new types of social collectives connected by online social interaction, revealing important information about their lives. Chapter "Migrants' Voices" is about rural-to-urban migration. It begins with a brief review of migration as a theme in writings about Badagas, and then describes interviews with rural-to-urban migrants in Bangalore to understand more about their experiences of leaving the Nilgiri Hills and living in the city. A key thrust of the chapter is changing notions of being Badaga as they engage the city, which is malleable and in a state of flux, and the ways by which people understand quality of life.

The final chapter concludes with a summary of the key findings of the research followed by a consideration of their limitations as well as directions for future studies.

References

Agesthialingom, S. (1972). Nouns of the Badaga language. *Journal of the American Oriental Society, 92*(2), 276–279.

Belli Gowder, M. (1923–1941). *A historical research on the hill tribes of the Nilgiris.* Unpublished manuscript, Ketti, Nilgiris District, India.

Belli Gowder, M. (1938–41). *Origin of the Badagas.* Unpublished manuscript, Ketti, Nilgiris District, India.

Benbow, J. (1930). *The Badagas–beliefs and customs.* Bangalore, India: United Theological College.

Bird-David, N. (1997). The Nilgiri tribal systems: A view from below. In P. Hockings (Ed.), *Blue mountains revisited: Cultural studies on the Nilgiri Hills* (pp. 5–22). New Delhi, India: Oxford University Press.

Breeks, J. W. (1873). *An account of the primitive tribes and monuments of the Nilagiris.* London, England: India Museum.

Congreve, H. (1847). The antiquities of the Neilgherry Hills, including an inquiry into the descent of the Thautawars or Todars. *Madras Journal of Literature and Science, 14*(1), 77–146.

Dirks, N. B. (2001). *Castes of mind: Colonialism and the making of modern India.* Princeton, NJ: Princeton University Press.

Emeneau, M. B. (1938). Toda culture thirty-five years after: An acculturation study. *Annals of the Bhandarkar Oriental Research Institute, 19*(2), 101–121.

Emeneau, M. B. (1939). The vowels of the Badaga language. *Language, 15*(1), 43–47.

Emeneau, M. B. (1944–1946). *Kota texts: Parts 1–4* (Vol. 2). Berkely, CA: University of California Press.

Emeneau, M. B. (1967). The south Dravidian languages. *Journal of the American Oriental Society, 87*(4), 365–413.

Emeneau, M. B. (1989). The languages of the Nilgiris. In P. Hockings (Ed.), *Blue Mountains: The ethnography and biogeography of a South Indian Region* (pp. 133–147). New Delhi, India: Oxford University Press.

Ferreira, J. (1603, April 1). A letter from Father Jacome Ferreira to the Vice-Provincial of Calicut.

Francis, W. (Ed.). (1908). *Madras district gazetteers: The Nilgiris.* Madras, India: Superintendent, Government Press.

Fry, D. P., Bonta, B. D., & Baszarkiewicz, K. (2008). Learning from extant cultures of peace. In J. De Rivera (Ed.), *Handbook on building cultures of peace* (pp. 11–26). New York, NY: Springer.

Gould, H. A. (1967). Priest and counterpriest: A structural analysis of Jajmani relationships in the Hindu Plains and the Nilgiri Hills. *Contributions to Indian Sociology, 1,* 28–57.

Grigg, H. B. (Ed.). (1880). *A manual of the Nilagiri district in the Madras presidency.* Madras, India: E. Keys, Government Press.

Harkness, H. (1832). *A description of a singular aboriginal race inhabiting the summit of the Neilgherry Hills, or Blue Mountains of Coimbatoor, in the southern peninsula of India.* London, England: Smith, Elder and Company.

Heidemann, F. (1997). Immigrant labourers and local networks in the Nilgiri. In P. Hockings (Ed.), *Blue mountains revisited: Cultural studies on the Nilgiri hills* (pp. 148–163). New Delhi, India: Oxford University Press.

Heidemann, F. (2014). Objectification and social aesthetics: Memoranda and the celebration of "Badaga Day". *Asian Ethnology, 73*(1/2), 91–109.

Hockings, P. (1968). Identity in complex societies: Are the Badagas caste or tribe? *Journal of African and Asian Studies, 2,* 29–35.

Hockings, P. (1975). Paikara: An iron age burial in South India. *Asian Perspectives, XVIII*(1), 26–50.

Hockings, P. (1980a). *Ancient Hindu refugees: Badaga social history, 1550–1975.* The Hague, The Netherlands: Mouton Publishers.

Hockings, P. (1980b). *Sex and disease in a mountain community.* New Delhi, India: Vikas Publishing House.

Hockings, P. (1982). Badaga kinship rules in their socio-economic context. *Anthropos, 77*(5/6), 851–874.

Hockings, P. (1988). *Counsel from the ancients: A study of Badaga proverbs, prayers, omens and curses.* Berlin, Germany: Mouton de Gruyter.

Hockings, P. (Ed.). (1989). *Blue Mountains: The ethnography and biogeography of a South Indian region.* New Delhi, India: Oxford University Press.

Hockings, P. (1993). Ethnic identity in a complex society: The Badaga case. *Bulletin of the National Museum of Ethnology, 18*(2), 347–364.

Hockings, P. (Ed.). (1997). *Blue mountains revisited: Cultural studies on the Nilgiri hills.* New Delhi, India: Oxford University Press.

Hockings, P. (1999). *Kindreds of the earth: Badaga household structure and demography.* New Delhi, India: SAGE Publications.

Hockings, P. (2008). All aboard the Nilgiri Express!—sustained links between anthropology and a single Indian district. *History and Anthropology, 19*(1), 1–16.

Hockings, P. (2013). *So long a saga: Four centuries of Badaga social history.* New Delhi, India: Manohar.

Hockings, P., & Pilot-Raichoor, C. (1992). *A Badaga-English dictionary.* Berlin, Germany: Mouton de Gruyter.

Kennedy, D. (1996). *The magic mountains: Hill stations and the British Raj.* Berkeley, CA: University of California Press.

King, W. R. (1870). The aboriginal tribes of the Nilgiri hills. *The Journal of Anthropology, 1*(1), 18–51.

Lehmann, H., & Cutbrush, M. (1952). Sickle-cell trait in southern India. *British Medical Journal, 23*(1), 404–405.

Mahias, M.-C. (1997). The construction of the Nilgiris as a 'tribal sanctuary'. In P. Hockings (Ed.), *Blue mountains revisited: Cultural studies on the Nilgiri hills* (pp. 316–334). New Delhi, India: Oxford University Press.

Mandelbaum, D. (1941). Culture change among the Nilgiri tribes. *American Anthropologist, 43*(1), 19–26.

Mandelbaum, D. G. (1955). The world and the world view of the Kota. In M. Marriott (Ed.), *Village India: Studies in the little community* (pp. 223–254). Chicago, IL: University of Chicago Press.

Mandelbaum, D. G. (1956). The Kotas in their social setting. In *Introduction to the civilization of India: Changing dimensions of Indian society and culture.* Chicago, IL: Syllabus Division, The College, The University of Chicago.

Mandelbaum, D. G. (1982). The Nilgiris as a region. *Economic & Political Weekly, 17*(36), 1459–1467.

Mandelbaum, D. G. (1989). The Nilgiris as a region. In P. Hockings (Ed.), *Blue mountains: The ethnography and biogeography of a South Indian region* (pp. 1–19). New Delhi, India: Oxford University Press.

Mantramurti, A. (1981). Traditional panchayat system of the Badagas of the Nilgiris. *The Indian Journal of Political Science, 42*(3), 48–61.

Marshall, W. E. (1873). *A Phrenologist amongst the Todas or the study of a primitive tribe in South India: History, character, customs, religion, infanticide, polyandry, language*. London, England: Longmans, Green, and Co.

Metz, F. (1864). *The tribes inhabiting the Neilgherry hills: Their social customs and religious rites*. Mangalore, India: Basel Mission Press.

Misra, R. (1972). Inter-tribal relations in Erumad. *The Eastern Anthropologist, 25*(2), 135–148.

Misra, P. K. (1999, December 14). The Badaga way of life. *The Hindu*.

Naik, I. A. R. (1966). *The culture of the Nilgiri Hills, with its catalogue collection at the British Museum* (Unpublished doctoral dissertation). University of London, England.

Neilson, J., & Pritchard, B. (2009). *Value chain struggles: Institutions and governance in the plantation districts of South India*. Sussex, England: Wiley.

Ouchterlony, J. (1868). *Geographical and statistical memoir of the Neilgherry mountains*. Madras, India: Higginbotham & Co.

Ranga, N. (1934). *The tribes of the Nilgiris: Their social and economic conditions*. Bezwada, India: Vani Press.

Rivers, W. H. R. (1906). *The Todas*. London, England: Macmillan and Co., Limited.

Thiagarajan, S. (2012, December 4). Badaga language not a dialect of Kannada, claims French linguistic scholar. *The Times of India*. Retrieved from http://timesofindia.indiatimes.com/city/coimbatore/Badaga-language-not-a-dialect-of-Kannada-claims-French-linguistic-scholar/articleshow/17472123.cms

Thurston, E., & Rangachari, K. (1909). *Castes and tribes of Southern India*. Madras, India: Government Press.

Vishwanathan, H., Edwin, D., Usharani, M. V., & Majumder, P. P. (2003). Insertion/deletion polymorphisms in tribal populations of Southern India and their possible evolutionary implications. *Human Biology, 75*(6), 873–887.

von Lengerke, H., & Blasco, F. (1989). The Nilgiri environment. In P. Hockings (Ed.), *Blue mountains: The ethnography and biogeography of a South Indian Region* (pp. 20–78). New Delhi, India: Oxford University Press.

Walker, A. R. (1986). *The Toda of South India: A new look*. New Delhi, India: Hindustan Publishing Corporation.

Walker, A. (1989). Toda society between tradition and modernity. In P. Hockings (Ed.), *Blue mountains: The ethnography and biogeography of a South Indian Region* (pp. 186–205). New Delhi, India: Oxford University Press.

Ward, B. (1821). Geographical and statistical memoir of a survey of the Neelgherry Mountains in the province of Coimbatore made in 1821 under the superintendence of Captain B. S. Ward, Deputy Surveyor-General. In H. B. Grigg (Ed.), *A Manual of the Nilagiri district in the Madras presidency* (lx–lxxviii). Madras, India: E. Keys, Government Press.

Whitehouse, T. (1873). *Lingerings of light in a dark land: Being researches into the past history and present condition of the Syrian Church of Malabar*. London, England: William Brown & Co.

Zagarell, A. (1997). The megalithic graves of the Nilgiri Hills and The Moyar Ditch. In P. Hockings (Ed.), *Blue mountains revisited: Cultural studies on the Nilgiri Hills* (pp. 23–73). New Delhi, India: Oxford University Press.

Methodology

Abstract This chapter describes the methodology of the monograph which includes multi-sited ethnography, thematic analysis, coding, and reflexivity, from a symbolic interactionist perspective. Each piece of the methodology is explained and justified. The chapter begins with an overview of the multiple fieldsites chosen to challenge the localisation of Badagas in the Nilgiri Hills in previous studies, understand people as dynamic, mobile, and multiply situated, and to capture new forms of identities and quality of life in flux and which transcend bounded spaces. The chapter continues with an outline of the theoretical orientation of the research, symbolic interactionism, employed to examine identities and shared experiences and meanings of Badagas in India with emphasis on agency, social process, and subjectivity, a deliberate move away from macro-level deterministic, functionalist, and structuralist thinking that is typical of previous work. Next is an outline of an investigation into subjective quality of life among Badagas from their own point of view, an approach hitherto neglected in the literature. The final section summarises the methods of data collection and analysis. This contemporary social constructionist approach irons out many of the epistemological problems in earlier writings.

Keywords Badagas · Bangalore · Internet forum · Multi-sited ethnography
Rural-to-urban migration

What does it mean to be a Badaga in India today, and how is it any different to being another person in the Nilgiris, South India, or beyond? How do Badagas live, and how is their quality of life? At first glance, answers to these questions might seem obvious and straightforward as the previous chapter reviews a rich literature about their culture and history, a working sense of who they are. But answers are not so simple if we take a step back and think in terms of human diversity, and Badagas as a large and diverse group of people engaging new social landscapes which influence how they communicate, interact, and understand life. Identity and quality of life are far more complex than portrayed in previous studies, and fresh thinking is needed to develop a more meaningful and sensitive conceptualisation of the Badaga category.

© The Author(s) 2018

27

G. Davey, *Quality of Life and Well-Being in an Indian Ethnic Community*,
SpringerBriefs in Well-Being and Quality of Life Research,
https://doi.org/10.1007/978-3-319-90662-1_2

To begin answering these questions, this chapter describes the methodology of the monograph which includes multi-sited ethnography, thematic analysis, coding, and reflexivity, from a symbolic interactionist perspective, complementary approaches focused on analytically disclosing the subjective knowledge and meaning-making of Badagas. Each aspect of the methodology is explained and justified below with clear reasons for its choice. The chapter begins with an overview of its multi-sited approach which was designed to overcome the limited conceptualisation of Badagas and the Nilgiri Hills in previous studies as local and bounded in an isolated region. It removes geographical barriers to understand people as dynamic, mobile, and multiply situated, to capture new forms of identities in flux which transcend bounded spaces. The chapter continues with an outline of the theoretical orientation of the research, symbolic interactionism. A symbolic interactionist perspective avoids the overly deterministic view that is typical of previous work, and enabled the author to examine Badagas on the basis of their own views. Next is an outline of an investigation of subjective quality of life among Badagas from their own point of view, an approach hitherto neglected in previous studies. The final section summarises the methods of data collection and analysis.

Fieldsites: Multi-sited Ethnography

Multi-sited ethnography was employed as both the methodological framework and final product of the research, namely this monograph. Multi-sited fieldwork has gained recognition in social science in response to a growing interest in fully appreciating contemporary issues such as advances in new media, movements of people, and relationships between local and global (Falzon 2009; Marcus 1995, 2011). It is a different standpoint to previous studies of Badagas which employed conventional ethnography and regarded people and culture as local and bounded in an isolated region, discussed in the previous chapter (Davey 2012a). A multi-sited approach was adopted in the research to lift Badagas out of their academic anchoring in a particular locality; as argued throughout this book, they cannot be appreciated by sole focus on distinctiveness and localisation in the Nilgiris, and assumptions that culture is an enclosed and self-constrained construct, as all places are connected in multifarious ways. They are moving around India and the world, and are multiply situated, and should be appreciated as a dynamic and mobile population. The 'natural habitat' of Badagas now includes the city and the Internet which have become important in their lives. Multi-sited ethnography was also suitable for the interdisciplinary nature of the research.

The research was about Badagas in urban areas—the online and offline inhabitants of Indian cities—and not people in the Nilgiri Hills, although they do make appearances. The primary fieldsites were an Internet forum and a city (Bangalore), chosen based on the research questions and opportunities for comparison, as discussed below. Yet while the monograph sometimes draws arbitrary lines between online and offline worlds, it is important to bear in mind a divide does not actually exist as people live concurrently in both. In addition to the primary fieldsites, parts of the research took place elsewhere, for example pilot work in the Nilgiris and an interview in Hong Kong, as the research also attended to the ways Badagas positioned themselves locally and globally.

The location of the first study was an Internet forum dedicated to Badagas, an online website with dialogues in the form of posted messages. It enabled them to share information and opinions through everyday conversations with like-minded people around India and the world, as it was a platform for communication. The study was primarily an investigation of the portrayal of quality of life and identities including how they were negotiated and developed through social media use, and the nature of the new type of online community, a lens through which to examine Badagas in contemporary India. The Internet forum, a fieldsite in which the author spent an extended period of time getting close to the community, was selected carefully based on a comprehensive computerised search of potential sites. A number of relevant sites were examined by reading messages and postings, and in some cases preliminary coding samples of discourse to narrow the choice. The site selected for the study appeared to be the most suitable and informative as forum posts suggested a sense of community and identification among contributors; also, it was easily and publically accessible at all times, and satisfied ethical considerations. It was a kind of community space primed to facilitate communication and connectedness between people, and a tool for storytelling and sharing experiences and knowledge. Unlike other types of social media such as Facebook and LinkedIn, which concern facilitating personal self-presentation, the Internet forum's interface catered for both individual and collective expression. It was also a source of information about the goings-on of Badagas and their past and current circumstances, and therefore was ideal for examining communication about identities and quality of life. The forum consisted of discussion boards onto which registered members posted messages in English subject to moderation, which anyone with an Internet connection and web browser could access. Forum members interacted with one another by clicking on and reading threads (textual conversations organized chronologically on webpages), and by adding their own voices to the conversations. Therefore, the study was essentially archival research of an existing public record of texts. The data were particularly valuable as they referred to personal writings from multiple viewpoints, subjective opinions of Badagas. As forum posts dated back a decade, another advantage was an opportunity to examine temporal themes, and the sample of participants in the forum is particularly noteworthy in terms of its size and representativeness of cities. The Internet study began in 2009, and continued to 2014.

The second study was conducted in Bangalore (Bengaluru) with rural-to-urban migrants to gain an appreciation of their experiences and what it means to be a Badaga in the city. Bangalore was the location of the study for several reasons (Davey 2012b). As the capital city of Karnataka State with a population of about 8.42 million, and a major economic centre in India with a leading role in the country's information technology sector, Bangalore is a major destination of Badagas and other migrant Indians; over two-thirds of the city's population are migrants. Therefore, it was a fitting location to study migrants. Also, Bangalore is an ethnically diverse city with a fusion of cultures and cosmopolitan lifestyles, a fertile ground for exploring identity and quality of life. During pilot research, I met migrants living and working in Bangalore, and they shared rich stories about their migration and lives, and confirmed that Bangalore was a popular choice for Badagas because of its economic opportunities and relatively close distance to the Nilgiri Hills. The participants of the study lived in a range of areas in the city, and they chose the location of their interviews (coffee shops, homes, and public places). The study began during a two-month residence in 2010, and continued with follow-up interviews in 2012 and 2013. In this study, migration is taken to mean the more-or-less permanent movement of individuals or groups from one area to another, examined from a social science perspective. Although the research focused on migrants born in the Nilgiri Hills (first-generation migrants), interviews were also conducted with two second-generation migrants to refine and saturate a theme in the emerging thematic analysis (rather than as a separate in-depth study of second-generation migrants), as detailed in Chapter "Migrants' Voices".

It is important to note from the outset that multi-sited ethnography is not the same as the classic research model of single-site ethnography. It is a new mode of ethnographic research that breaks convention, and, in many respects, challenges the status quo (Falzon 2009; Marcus 1995, 2011; Hannerz 2003). There is no descriptive or theoretical prescription, and even conventional ethnography now has different connotations—both are eclectic methodologies. The design, structure, and form of my ethnographic research remains individual and personal, derived from the research itself rather than a priori knowledge, as its contours emerged during research across multiple sites on topics that turned out to be relevant in the lives of Badagas. Thus the research topics and methodology were not pre-determined by a recipe but an evolving process which required methods that escaped the boundaries of the fixed.

Social Identity and Symbolic Interactionism

Writings about identity are sprinkled on almost all topics of social science, and some scholars have even called for the concept to be abandoned as it has become unworkable (Brubaker and Cooper 2000). Though the burgeoning literature is remarkable and often enlightening, its scope and complexity certainly pose a challenge for the present study; also, as the previous chapter shows, identity has been applied widely, loosely, and in contradictory ways in writings about the Nilgiris with no clear definition or conceptualization. Therefore, my research must, by necessity, be selective. With this in mind, the research is situated within the sociological approach to identity (symbolic interactionism), a major perspective that underlies a great deal of interest in the topic, and is introduced in the following paragraphs.

In general terms, identity studies align with either classical essentialist perspectives characterised by rigidity and structural and institutional forces, or contemporary social constructionist perspectives which emphasise dynamic and fluid natures of identities beset with contradiction and contestation, constantly evolving as meanings are negotiated and revised by people. The former characterises previous studies of

Badagas, reviewed in Chapter "Introduction", which do not capture the complexity of being Badaga and the extent to which it is played out, both in theoretical and practical terms. This monograph draws on social constructionism which underscores recent work in sociology on cosmopolitan and multicultural identities in which ideas of rigid group boundaries have given way to fluidity and hybridity. Extreme versions of constructionism, associated with postmodernism, envisage identity as ambiguously defined, inherently performative, and transient and continuously changing; some scholars even consider it to be a purely theoretical construct imposed on the social world.

Sociological approaches to identity originated in the United States around 1870 in philosophical ideas about pragmatism advocated by John Dewey, William James, Sanders Peirce, and James Tufts, and were advanced in the classic works of early modern social science by Charles Cooley, William James, and George Mead, to name a few (Cooley 1902; Mead 1934). For example, James's (1890) analyses of multiple social selves, and Cooley's (1902) looking glass self, which both refer to identities shaped by social context and perceptions of others, are well known to social scientists. American sociologist George Mead is credited as the founder of symbolic interactionism. Mead's theory of the mind and self, the notion that self emerges out of social process, was a major contribution to understanding identity. *Mind, Self and Society* (1934) details Mead's conceptions of the social self, how the mind and self cannot be understood as independent of sociality. Communication, forms of symbolic (social) interaction, take place via shared symbols (definitions, gestures, language, and rituals), and presuppose a social context within which people interact, giving rise to meanings. In other words, there is no meaning of an object independent of the individual and their social world. In contrast to functionalism and previous studies of the Nilgiris, symbolic interactionism contends the self is not mechanistic or structurally determined but a flexible structure of human experience that arises through interpretation and negotiation in response to other people and their intersubjective relations. Self emerges out of "a special set of social relations with everyone involved in a specific social project" (Mead 1934, p. 156). Mead also developed ideas about distinctions between two aspects of self, 'I' and 'me', as self is an active response to the social rather than a passive reflection of it, a dialectical relationship between the individual and society. Mead's social philosophy is also elaborated in *The Philosophy of the Act* (1938).

Another prominent perspective was advocated by Herbert Blumer at the University of Chicago, also known as the Chicago School. Blumer, in a series of articles and other works brought together in his book *Symbolic Interactionism* (1969), coined and developed 'symbolic interactionism' as a cohesive theory with specific methodological implications. Blumer's symbolic interactionism centres on the processes people use to constantly create and recreate experiences in dynamic social interaction, the construction and negotiation of social realities by social actors as core elements of communication (Blumer 1969). Echoing Mead, Blumer posited that individuals have a self, something which they make of themselves, and that identity refers to the labels that one attributes to self and associated social expectations through collective and individual action. Self is also regarded as a reflexive process, as the individual actively interprets objects in the world and does not merely respond in an automatic manner. Society, viewed through the lens of symbolic interactionism, is an outgrowth of communication and social interaction based on meanings; and, reciprocally, society is basic to the development of self as social interaction shapes society which then plays back on social interaction and self, each constitutive of the other. Self and society are continuously being created and recreated during ongoing social interaction as common meanings are developed and manipulated by those engaged in it. Self and society, then, are pluralistic and reciprocal. Stryker's (2000) work, referred to as the Indiana School or 'structural symbolic interactionism', bridges gaps between micro- and macro-concerns, and counters critiques of symbolic interactionism's neglect of social structure and broader societal issues. Following in these footsteps of earlier pioneers, the work of many other scholars has since advanced a number of developments in symbolic interactionism and identity, and a review is beyond the scope of this ethnography.

These tenets make symbolic interactionism a suitable starting point for investigating the lives of Badagas in the twenty first century. However, it is necessary to tighten up the conceptualization of identity in this monograph. From a symbolic interactionist viewpoint, intersections of differences such as culture and ethnicity are important sources of identity. Unlike previous structural functionalist analyses of Badaga society, the present research, based on symbolic interactionism, shifts the focus to micro-level processes and the capacity of each individual to act independently with distinct interpretations and life journeys, and to respond reflexively to coordinate with and anticipate others. Meanings such as 'Badaga' and 'quality of life' are not inherent but constantly perceived, negotiated, and reinterpreted among people in an interactive process of shared conscious action as people interact, and, therefore, are constantly in flux. In the research described here, while macrotheoretical concepts are acknowledged, the connotations of identity and quality of life are not assumed to be inherent in but products of intersubjective processes among those who regard themselves as defined by similarity and difference. Consequently, Badaga identities and lives are not concrete, structured, patterned, or stable, as assumed in the literature, but dynamic and constantly in flux, which gives rise to the possibility of multiple understandings of self. The focus of the research, then, is an exploration of life as it is interpreted by Badagas rather than the theoretical and social orientations of previous writings by British colonists and anthropologists. The stance that the individual is the arbiter of their identities gains credence from the almost universally accepted notion that groups defined by difference are intrinsically socially constructed and subjective (Aspinall 1997; Bradby 2003; Maleševic 2004; Smith 2002). Based on this premise, the following chapters report an investigation of lay beliefs of identity and life quality among Badagas (common sense understandings of 'ordinary' people), and their basis in the various micro- and macro-level factors which constitute the fabric of daily life and society. They can be contrasted with the theoretical and professional views of academics and professionals reviewed in Chapter "Introduction". This book can also be regarded as a desire to establish good practice in researching indigenous people in the Nilgiris and India by avoiding self-serving and oppressive ideologies, a call for greater sensitivity. Moreover, by aligning the methodology with symbolic interactionism, it is possible to acknowledge the interaction between the researcher and researched and its influence on the construction of the findings of the monograph, discussed in the final chapter.

As being Badaga has real-life relevance to the ways people experience and understand the world, a middle-path approach is adopted here which takes, as a starting point, the importance of guarding against reifying the notion of a social category while also recognising it has meanings to people who self-identify as such. A contradiction in this starting point is that adoption of the category 'Badaga' seems to support the idea of boundaries which reify its separateness (Aspinall 1997; Brubaker and Cooper 2000; Smith 2002). Paradoxically, the ethnography, as an investigation of a social category, reifies an identity by drawing a boundary around its existence, a symbolic declaration of distinction to others, while also claiming to critique and resolve the simple portrayal of cultural essentialism and fixity in the literature. Even so, there are several important justifications. As the overarching aim of the monograph is to review representations of Badagas in the literature, at least some kind of foundation of self is needed as a basis of comparability and consistency, especially when undertaking a secondary analysis of previous studies. Pilot work undertaken by the author in the Nilgiri Hills revealed popular usage of the category, as it constitutes appropriate terminology from the viewpoint of people, something real and important to them. Although 'Badaga' came into existence through a process of category formation by Westerners in European discovery and colonialism, these constructed identities have been internalized by the local people. As the sociologist William Isaac Thomas observed, if people believe a thing to be real, then it is real in its consequences for them.

Therefore, it is important to recognise it is double-edged, not as a matter of intellectual sloppiness but as tensions between essentialist and constructivist approaches in producing fixed identity categories that are inherently complex and variable. As Brubaker and Cooper (2000) argue, the prevailing constructivist stance on identity stipulates it is ambiguous, constructed, fluid, and multiple, which leaves no rationale for conceptualizing identity at all; if it is fluid, how can we understand it as a hard, crystallised concept? While it might seem sensible to throw away the label 'Badaga' and other imposed categories, doing so might have meant the participants gave complex and diverse beliefs that could not be brought together for the aims of the research, as noted in studies about ethnicity in censuses. The middle path approach of the ethnography attempts to weigh up these issues by acknowledging the problematic usage of the label while concurrently accepting it as an analytical category as a prelude to making sense of a loosely connected group of people in India. It should be accepted for what it is: An initial simplified and generalised stereotype reported in the literature which paves the way to delve further into the complexity of Badaganess in all its possibilities. Thus the term 'Badaga' was applied loosely as an ice-breaker, as the participants in the research were asked to categorise and self-assign aspects of their own sense of self to mitigate these categorisation difficulties, for example by permitting fluid and hybrid identities to be expressed.

Quality of Life

The above reasoning also applies to investigating quality of life of Badagas. The literature reviewed in Chapter "Introduction" is dated and spotty and portrays both positive and negative depictions of life quality which need to be elucidated. Also, in the literature, quality of life is a broad, multidimensional concept, and researchers have proposed different definitions and approaches (Cummins 1996, 2000; Selin and Davey 2012; Sirgy et al. 2006). Indeed, the term has become a catch-all which is elusive and difficult to pin down—a clear, precise, and agreed definition appears to be absent from the literature. Therefore, it is necessary to clarify its denotation in this monograph.

Social scientists have made invaluable contributions to quality of life in many contexts; almost all social science deals with it in some way, and it is the desired outcome of social policies (Ferriss 2004; Sirgy et al. 2006; Selin and Davey 2012). Precursors of quality of life research in early modern social science were concerned with views on morality, society, and social progress (Veenhoven 2000). Notable early contributions include the works of Auguste Comte, Émile Durkheim, and Georg Simmel which interpreted the social problems of their time (Veenhoven 2000). Quality of life has also been a topic of interest in philosophy, which shows it is as old as civilization, although philosophical contributions tend to be speculative (Sirgy et al. 2006).

While people's living conditions have been a concern of social science since its beginnings, 'quality of life' as a term or concept per se was not considered until recently. In one of the first analyses of quality of life in a sociology journal, Gerson (1976) interpreted it as an elaboration of Mead's (1934) ideas of self and society, which he likened to individual and community quality of life respectively. The former, according to Gerson, stresses an individual's freedom and achievement, and their dominance over society, despite imposed constraints. The 'natural law' and 'natural rights' philosophy, which advances certain rights or values as inherent by virtue of human nature, and upon which American political theory was initially based, is a preeminent example of an individualist approach to quality of life, evidenced by the works of classical theorists including John Locke, Thomas Jefferson, William Blackstone, and Adam Smith. Community quality of life, in contrast, is a transcendental approach concerning the extent to which the individual carries out their place in the larger social order and in the interests of society at-large, a primacy of the social over the individual. Gerson emphasised interaction of self and society, and cautioned against attempts to dichotomise 'individual' and 'society'.

Despite Gerson's attempts to spark interest in quality of life among sociologists, his ideas were not taken further. A decade later, Schuessler and Fisher's (1985) extensive review of the status of quality of life research found it had seldom entered the literature; and Sociological Abstracts first used it as a category of sociological research in 1979. Yet, several components of quality of life figured prominently, albeit under other rubrics, notably the 'good life' and 'happiness'. Two decades later, Ferriss (2004) re-examined the presence of quality of life research in sociology, and concluded it was still largely missing from the literature, although studies frequently address its components. However, these conclusions—that quality of life as a concept is not commonly taken up in sociology, and that few sociologists have recognised its value—might be an artefact of the ways different writers socially construct academic disciplines and fields with arbitrary and narrow boundaries and terminologies, as sociological contributions are not always distinguishable in interdisciplinary writings. The assumption that purely sociological contributions are difficult to isolate (Ferriss 2004; Schuessler and Fisher 1985) depends on the construction of sociology as an academic discipline, which differs among people, time, and countries. Indeed, the types of research now conducted under the banner of quality of life research were actually being done by earlier generations of sociologists but perhaps under other labels or in cognate disciplines.

Quality of life research gained momentum in the last century in reports by governments and organizations. In the 1930s, sociologists were instrumental in advancing quantitative measures and reports of living standards, and examples include Chapin (1933), Sewell (1940), Odum (1936), Cottam and Mangus (1942), as reviewed by Ferriss (2004) and Sirgy et al. (2006). Efforts to collect and organise data became more systematic around the 1960s with funding and support by governments and prominent sociologists (Bauer 1966; Ferriss 2004; Sirgy et al. 2006). As a research focus, it became known collectively as the social indicators movement which measured social indicators in survey questions to evaluate individual, family, community, regional, and national circumstances in a range of areas—crime, environment, health, housing, and so on. Social indicators are measures of people's perceptions of their living circumstances, and can be used to evaluate how people's lives are going, proxies for quality of life and social welfare; a wide range of variables have been measured and studied. The social indicators movement gradually became institutionalized with landmarks, especially the launch of the journal *Social Indicators Research* in the 1970s, and the founding of the *International Society for Quality of Life Studies* in the 1990s, alongside developments in empirical measurements of life satisfaction (Andrews and Withey 1976; Campbell et al. 1976; Ferriss 2004; Land 1983; Schuessler and Fisher 1985; Sirgy et al. 2006; Veenhoven 2000). In social science, quality of life research largely arose out of the social indicators movement. Its growth was fuelled in part by dissatisfaction with the priority of economic indicators and with economic growth following the post-war economic boom. Appreciation of people's judgments of their circumstances rather than only those of academics, economists, policymakers, and other experts, and mounting evidence of discrepancies between objective and subjective life quality, were also important (Cummins 1995, 1996; Diener and Seligman 2004; Sirgy et al. 2006; Land 1996). Research on subjective quality of life appreciates that people react differently to the same circumstances based on their personal attributes and experiences, and also recognises the value of the individual.

The above summary shows that quality of life research is fairly new and interdisciplinary, and consists of numerous overlapping directions. There are diverse views, conceptual approaches, and research methodologies concerning 'quality of life' in academic and popular writings, an eclectic pursuit. In this monograph I define quality of life as an umbrella concept to represent in general terms the wellbeing of Badagas and their community, the circumstances in which they live, and their understanding of those circumstances—being well physically, psychologically, and materially. The definition served as a starting point on which Badagas could build with their own interpretations. One stance in the literature, which is adopted in this ethnography, is to differentiate between objective and subjective quality of life (Cummins 2000; Davey et al. 2009). The former represents tangible criteria such as standard of living and income which are measured independently by experts, whereas the latter is a more personal evaluation by people under study of how life is going and the circumstances in which they live, subjective appraisals including beliefs, emotions, feelings, opinions, perceptions, and life experiences and histories, substantiated on interaction between the external conditions of life and internal perceptions of those conditions (Cummins 1995, 1996, 2000; Sirgy et al. 2006). Subjective quality of life can also be regarded as subjective well-being, a concept concerned with a person's evaluations of life. For example, whereas previous studies of Badagas tend to regard tangible measures such as standard of living as indicative of quality of life, my research is concerned with the individual's perceptions of those circumstances, since 'objective' measures are actually a product of the capacity to experience the world. Thus this monograph examines subjective quality of life among Badagas—their own interpretations of life and circumstances—an approach hitherto neglected in the literature. It addresses several limitations of previous studies of Badagas and India generally.

Much of the research on Badagas and in India relies on data collected with survey questions. Quality of life research paints a colourful picture of people's perceptions of life in the country and around the world and its determinants and mediators (Davey and Rato 2012; Rato and Davey 2012). Surveys such as the Gallup World Poll and World Values Survey (WVS), for example, show that people in India score just above average on a wide range of social indicators, and urban residents report higher scores than rural residents; although not as high as in many other countries, the scores are positioned in the positive range, and indicate the Indian population is generally satisfied with life (Biswas-Diener et al. 2012; Chen and Davey 2008). When data from various countries are ranked from lowest to highest, India is in the middle to lower portion as people in more industrialized countries report higher scores, and some Indian respondents report challenges and inadequate resources, e.g. food, shelter, and unemployment (Biswas-Diener et al. 2012). Indeed, differences in subjective wellbeing between countries are, to a large extent, explained by the wealth of nations (Diener et al. 1995), although scores also differ when income is controlled in statistical models. However, the tendency to appraise cultures and societies based on statistical analyses of survey scores raises critical questions about appropriateness. Another limitation of country comparisons is the assumption that India is a single cultural entity, which overlooks cultural heterogeneity of the country as well as similarities and cultural influences which extend beyond its national borders in the globalising world. There is only a nascent literature on the quality of life of smaller communities in India (Biswas-Diener et al. 2012; Davey et al. 2009; Selin and Davey 2012), which justifies the present study of Badagas. The good life, subjective and culture-bound, does not mean the same for all people, and it has even been suggested its conceptualisation might be an artefact invented by social scientists (Mathews and Izquierdo 2010). While a handful of studies have investigated economic and living standards (objective quality of life) among Badagas, as revealed in the previous chapter, there has been no consideration of the views of the people (subjective quality of life), in line with previous conventions in social science such as structural determinism and functionalism. Even after many years of research, a scholar commented "the goals of daily action are not often stated, and have to be inferred from what people are seen to do and heard to say in conversation. It is difficult to be sure that the pursuit of happiness, so widely valued in our modern world, is perceived as a worthwhile goal by the Badagas" (Hockings 1989, p. 209). This passing comment is a clear example of neglect by scholars of the subjective side of life, as research has only attended to objective aspects. Yet the changes taking place in India and among Badagas are not simply about economic standards, as often assumed in writings, but also a cultural and personal process involving people and their lived experiences and constructions of change envisaged within their local settings. In other words, quality of life and identity are not objective or universal but actively constructed and produced by people, established on their judgements of social reality. Therefore, the thrust of this ethnography is to examine Badagas' own opinions which are important to them, attention to subjectivity, an approach hitherto neglected in previous studies. The ethnography fills a void in the literature by examining the human experience of being Badaga in contemporary India, an appreciation of the ways people define and think about themselves, and the ways they make sense of their lives and changing circumstances, to determine what it really stands for. From this perspective, the Badaga is the storyteller of quality of life, and not the scholar, which broadens the scope of the literature.

Data

The research reported in this book was approved by the Faculty of Social Science, The University of Kent. The Internet study was an unobtrusive analysis of a public space accessible by anyone with an Internet connection. Forum posts were primarily archival data consisting of computer-mediated communication, and thus the study was essentially archival research of an existing public record of texts. The researcher visited the website regularly over several years to investigate specific aspects of forum members' lives and their embeddedness in a wider set of circumstances. The dataset comprised more than 1500 posts written in English, and was amenable to inductive thematic analysis. Conversations in the forum were sequential, chronological narratives connected through a timeline in the order in which they occurred, a chronology of posts and social interactions in linear sequences from past to present (they were also located temporally to specific times and dates in the real word by time-stamped headers, and some messages by their references to events occurring in the real-world). Other types of communication in the Internet forum (audio, audiovisual, graphical, textual) were also considered when relevant to the research, for example hyperlinked websites, audio information (e.g. iTunes), visual information (e.g. Flickr), and audio-visual information (e.g. YouTube). Spam and unsolicited messaging was excluded from the analysis, and the amount was low and did not interfere with online conversations. An unobtrusive approach was taken as the researcher was not involved in creating or prompting posts, and did not reply to members, post messages, or contribute to their activities. The decision to be a non-participant was considered cautiously, and seemed appropriate as the data were primarily archival interactions. Ethical issues applicable to Internet methodology were also well-thought-out.

In the second study, in Bangalore, a sample of 24 Badagas was selected by convenience and purposive sampling, initiated through contacts made in earlier trips to the Nilgiri Hills. Ethnographic interviewing was employed to gather detailed information. It is set apart from other interviewing styles commonly used in research for several reasons (Skinner 2012). For example, it was conducted over time, and preceded with extensive preparatory work including trips and pilot work in Bangalore and the Nilgiris when I lived with Badagas and established connections with potential participants. The interviews were conducted during a lengthy residence in the city, and continued with follow up meetings, theoretical sampling, and respectful, long-term relationships. The participants had freedom to decide the information to share, as questions and topics were flexible and open-ended, and the interviewing method also took account of interviewer/interviewee co-production of knowledge. Therefore, the interviewing heard from Badagas directly to understand the complexity, nuances, and particularities of their lives from their perspectives. The sample consisted of only men as they represented the vast majority of rural-to-urban migrants. Each participant satisfied the following inclusion criteria: (i) identified himself as Badaga; (ii) born in the Nilgiri Hills, and brought up in an agricultural background; (iii) within the age-range 18–65 years (working adult); (iv) able to converse verbally in English; and (v) gave informed verbal consent to participate in the study. Also, to minimize confounding, the research primarily concerned Badagas from the upper portion of the Nilgiri Hills to the east (Nilgiri Plateau), as some scholars believe they differ to people in other areas. The average age of the sample was 35 years, and half of the participants were in the age-range 18–30 years as they were easier to recruit (the majority of migrants seemed to be young men). Two-thirds of the sample had completed secondary school, and one-third tertiary education. The interviewees were employed in a range of professional occupations in the city (business, civil service, education, engineering, and finance). Sample size was determined by data saturation as sampling of participants ceased when dimensions and gaps in each theme of the analysis had been explicated. Purposive and theoretical sampling was employed, facilitated by concurrent data collection and analysis. The thrust of theoretical sampling was follow-up interviews with participants via telephone and Skype, and recruitment of two new participants, to probe topics apparent in the initial analysis. Although the research focused on migrants born in the Nilgiri Hills (first-generation migrants), two second-generation migrants were interviewed in Bangalore and Hong Kong to gain insights into their lives.

The interviews took place in the participants' preferred settings rather than a university, and we met for several hours according to their preferences. To establish empathy and rapport, they commenced with an introduction and warm-up chat followed by guiding questions based on the theoretical direction of the study: What is your background and current situation? How do you identify yourself, and how do others identify you? What sorts of things come to mind when you think of being Badaga? How do you see yourself as Badaga with the knowledge that some people in the city are similar or different? What personal and social factors influence you being Badaga? How is your life and quality of life in the city? What aspects of city life do you like and dislike? Are you happy in Bangalore? The concept of boundaries was used as an analytical tool to understand the changeability of identities; a 'boundary' refers to distinctions constructed by the participants to separate and categorize themselves and others based on feelings of similarity, difference, and group membership. We discussed their perceptions of any boundaries in their social lives including their characteristics, conditions in which they existed, permeability, and boundary-work. Standardised interview questions were kept to a minimum and broached loosely to explore the men's own viewpoints without overly directing predetermined topics. These questions, and follow-up questions in response to initial replies, explored how the migrants understood and thought about self, their sense of identities in rural and urban areas in relation to social others, quality of life, and the processes which shaped them. In doing so, the findings paint a comprehensive picture of what it means to be a Badaga in modern-day India among migrants who departed their villages in the Nilgiri Hills to live and work in the city.

Since the approach diverges from the assumptions and practices of the classic model of single-site ethnography (Davey 2012a), it is instructive to reflect on its value and also to counter potential critiques of readers. Multi-sited ethnography tends to be more dependent on interviews, largely because of the time factor (Hannerz 2003), so the methodology described here is not unusual. The utility of interviews in social science is by no means uncritical, but there is a developing home for ethnographies that engage strongly with interviewing as a research method (Skinner 2012; Smith et al. 2015). Yet there are several other features which distinguish it from simple one site interviews with men in cities, and a one site analysis of an Internet forum. As a multi-sited ethnography, it is designed around a juxtaposition of locations, and with an explicit posited logic of connection (city residence), as all of the Badagas in Bangalore and the Internet forum were resident outside the Nilgiri Hills, and their identities and life quality were framed in that context. Therefore, it is an interconnection of sites, and the findings of both studies are woven together. Unlike conventional ethnography, participant observation was not possible in Bangalore as Badagas are dispersed in the city, and do not live in a community (in any case, defining the community as a fluid notion, one that takes shape in the realm of discourse, is in line with the premise of this monograph which tries to move away from bounded notions of culture). Accordingly, the project involved rigorous ethnographic work that reflected today's complex global context in which Badagas find themselves.

In both studies of the multi-sited ethnography, the data were analysed by coding and inductive thematic analysis, a widely-used qualitative approach. The dataset of each study was analysed separately to produce themes which characterized either the forum posts or fieldnotes from Bangalore. During pre-coding, each dataset was read carefully numerous times to appreciate their breadth and depth and highlight patterns of potential interest. It was followed by an in-depth coding process whereby each dataset was read and searched numerous times to identify and sort similarities and reoccurrences in the participants' discussions (codes), repeated patterns of meaning which captured something important to the overall research questions as descriptive or explanatory ideas. Initial coding involved analysing the conversations by line, sentence, and paragraph, breaking down data to discrete parts for close examination and comparison. A preliminary coding schema with 'codes' (essence-capturing, salient, summative, and repeated patterns relevant to the research), was then subjected to further analysis which included grouping codes as broader 'categories' and then 'themes' by identifying significant broader patterns of meaning, and fitting categories with one another to develop a coherent conceptual synthesis, the development of major themes in the data. It involved collating, linking, and integrating connotations and explanations during category development; constant comparison of codes and categories; and refinement and review of candidate codes, categories, and themes based on conceptual or thematic similarity. In summary, collections of codes were divided and grouped into core topics (categories) which were linked and integrated (themes) to consolidate and develop explanation. The coding process was recursive throughout these steps with concurrent data collection and analysis, and also reflexive as decisions were considered carefully. All coding was done manually using the paper-and-pen technique, coding by hand without assistance of a software program; although the datasets were large, it enabled closeness. The themes, when compared and consolidated with each other, furnished a rich picture of collective interpretation and action which took into account individuals and their social and historical settings, discussed in Chapters "Badagas Going Digital" and "Migrants' Voices" with illustrative data extracts and analyst narrative.

A possible criticism is whether multi-sited ethnography produces the same quality of data as conventional ethnography. While it is true the type of data generated is different to single-site research, it is not necessarily in terms of quality (Falzon 2009). For example, although the time I spent in Bangalore was relatively brief, around two months, it was preceded with extensive preparatory work including trips and pilot work in Bangalore and the Nilgiris, and continued with follow up meetings and theoretical sampling. Moreover, the online discussions analysed in Chapter "Badagas Going Digital" date back more than a decade, more than 2000 A4 pages when saved as text-readable files (single-spaced, 12-point font). The rich information seems equivalent in depth to the corpus expected of classic Malinowskian fieldwork, and is much more substantive than other qualitative methodologies which often involve shorter data collection and analysis. In common with other examples of multi-sited ethnography, it retains in-depth knowledge yet focuses on specific topics and multiple sites. It was based on the need to reform the deeply engrained mind-set and culture of previous researchers investigating people in the Nilgiris. I do not claim to have a grasp of the entire lives of Badagas, as the aims of the research were to explore specific aspects of their lives. In any case, it is inappropriate here to think of space- and time-frames as criteria of research quality as the sites and topics studied were markedly different to the Nilgiri Hills, for example the Internet forum was actually a reconceptualization of time and space as well as what counts as a research site, an alternative way of structuring Badaga sociality and research (Hallett and Barber 2014). The inclusion of an online space in the research can be regarded as its strength because studies of the Nilgiri Hills have overlooked the importance of new media. These challenges are not specific to this monograph but a reflection of how a multi-sited study differs from the single site study of a twentieth century anthropologist.

Concluding Summary

This chapter is a review of the research methodology including its guiding approaches and theoretical framework. It answers three main questions: How were the data obtained? How were they interpreted? And, what reasons justify the methodology? The first section overviewed the multi-sited framework of the research and its departure from previous single-site studies of indigenous people in the Nilgiri Hills, to explore present-day issues (migration, and new media usage) embedded within a complex and globalising India. The intention was to avoid culture-bound misapprehensions associated with the ethnographic style of earlier work. The next section overviewed the theoretical orientation of the research, symbolic interactionism, and social constructionist epistemology, which was employed to examine shared understandings and experiences among Badagas, a deliberate move away from macro-level and functionalist standpoints. The remaining sections of the chapter described the conceptualisation of identity and quality of life in the research; data collection involving online forum posts and face-to-face interviews; and thematic analysis and coding. Anticipated challenges in the research design, for example tensions between essentialist and constructivist approaches, were considered. The methodology, then, was an interpretative group of complementary methods—multi-sited ethnography, symbolic interactionism, thematic analysis, and reflexivity. It provided flexibility in approaching identity and quality of life as dynamic and constantly in flux. While the literature and macrotheoretical concepts were acknowledged, meanings of objects were not assumed to be inherent or fixed but the product of intersubjective processes among those who self-identified as Badaga based on similarity and difference. Based on this methodology, Chapters "Badagas Going Digital" and "Migrants' Voices" explore the identities and life quality of Badagas in two connected locations, the first online in an Internet forum, and the second in the real world in Bangalore. Specifically, the next chapter explores the online portrayal of Badagas and their lives. It begins with a note on the paucity of media and visual studies of the Nilgiris, the need for further research, and the role of media as a prime information source and facilitator of cultural and identity change. Next is an analysis of online discussions in an Internet forum, a source of information about the goings-on of Badagas including their past and current circumstances, as a prelude to Chapter "Migrants' Voices".

References

Andrews, F., & Withey, S. (1976). *Social indicators of well-being: Americans' perceptions of life quality*. New York, NY: Plenum Press.

Aspinall, P. J. (1997). The conceptual basis of ethnic group terminology and classifications. *Social Science and Medicine, 45*(5), 689–98.

Bauer, R. (Ed.). (1966). *Social indicators*. Cambridge, MA: The MIT Press.

Biswas-Diener, R., Tay, L., & Diener, E. (2012). Happiness in India. In H. Selin & G. Davey (Eds.), *Happiness across cultures: Views of happiness and quality of life in non-western cultures* (pp. 125–140). Dordrecht, The Netherlands: Springer.

Blumer, H. (1969). *Symbolic interactionism: Perspective and method*. Berkeley, CA: University of California Press.

Bradby, H. (2003). Describing ethnicity in health research. *Ethnicity & Health, 8*(1), 5–13.

Brubaker, R., & Cooper, F. (2000). Beyond "identity". *Theory and Society, 29*(1), 1–47.

Campbell, A., Converse, P., & Rogers, W. (1976). *The quality of American life: Perceptions, evaluations, and satisfactions*. New York, NY: Russell Sage Foundation.

Chapin, F. S. (1933). *The measurement of social status by the use of the Social Status Scale 1933*. Minneapolis, MN: The University of Minnesota Press.

Chen, Z., & Davey, G. (2008). Normative life satisfaction in Chinese societies. *Social Indicators Research, 89*(3), 557–564.

Cooley, C. H. (1902). *Human nature and the social order*. New York, NY: Charles Scribner's Sons.

Cottam, H., & Mangus, A. R. (1942). Standard of living: An empirical test of a definition. *Rural Sociology, 7*(4), 395–403.

Cummins, R. A. (1995). On the trail of the gold standard for subjective well-being. *Social Indicators Research, 35*(2), 179–200.

Cummins, R. A. (1996). The domains of life satisfaction: An attempt to order chaos. *Social Indicators Research, 38*(3), 303–328.

Cummins, R. A. (2000). Objective and subjective quality of life: An interactive model. *Social Indicators Research, 52*(1), 55–72.

Davey, G., Chen, Z., & Lau, A. (2009). Peace in a thatched hut—That is happiness: Subjective wellbeing among peasants in rural China. *Journal of Happiness Studies, 10*(2), 239–252.

Davey, G. (2012a). Anthropology. In S. Danver (Ed.), *Native Peoples of the World: An Encyclopedia of Groups, Cultures and Contemporary Issues* (pp. 705-707). Armonk, NY: M.E. Sharpe.

Davey, G. (2012b). Bangalore: 1900 to present. In A. Stanton., E. Ramsamy., P. Seybolt., & C. Elliott (Eds.), *Cultural sociology of the Middle East, Asia, & Africa: An encyclopedia (pp. IV165–IV167)*. Thousand Oaks, CA: SAGE Publications.

Davey, G., & Rato, R. (2012). Subjective wellbeing in China: A review. *Journal of Happiness Studies, 13*(2), 333–346.

Diener, E., & Seligman, M. E. P. (2004). Beyond money: Toward an economy of well-being. *Psychological Science in the Public Interest, 5*(1), 1–31.

Diener, E., Diener, M., & Diener, C. (1995). Factors predicting the subjective well-being of nations. *Journal of Personality and Social Psychology, 69*(5), 851–64.

Falzon, M.-A. (Ed.). (2009). *Multi-sited ethnography: Theory, praxis and locality in contemporary research*. Surrey, England: Ashgate.

Ferriss, A. (2004). The quality of life concept in sociology. *The American Sociologist, 35*(3), 37–51.

Gerson, E. M. (1976). On "Quality of Life". *American Sociological Review, 41*(5), 793–806.

Hallett, R. E., & Barber, K. (2014). Ethnographic Research in a Cyber Era. *Journal of Contemporary Ethnography, 43*(3), 306–330.

Hannerz, U. (2003). Being there…and there…and there! Reflections on multi-site ethnography. *Ethnography, 4*(2), 201–216.

Hockings, P. (Ed.). (1989). *Blue mountains: The ethnography and biogeography of a South Indian region*. New Delhi, India: Oxford University Press.

James, W. (1890). *The principles of psychology*. New York, NY: Henry Holt & Co., Publishers.

Land, K. C. (1983). Social indicators. *Annual Review of Sociology, 9,* 1–26.

Land, K. C. (1996). Social indicators and the quality of life: Where do we stand in the mid-1990s? *SINET: Social Indicators Network News, 45,* 5–8.

Maleševic, S. (2004). *The sociology of ethnicity.* London, England: SAGE Publications.

Marcus, G. E. (1995). Ethnography in/of the world system: The emergence of multi-sited ethnography. *Annual Review of Anthropology, 24,* 95–117.

Marcus, G. E. (2011). Mulit-sited ethnography: Five or six things I know about it now. In S. Coleman & P. von Hellermann (Eds.), *Problems and Possibilities in the translocation of research methods.* London, England: Routledge.

Mathews, G., & Izquierdo, C. (Eds.). (2010). *Pursuits of happiness: Well-being in anthropological perspective.* New York, NY: Berghahn Books.

Mead, G. H. (1934). *Mind, self, and society from the standpoint of a social behaviorist.* Chicago, IL: University of Chicago Press.

Mead, G. H. (1938). *The philosopy of the act.* Chicago, IL: University of Chicago Press.

Odum, H. N. (1936). *Southern regions of the United States.* Chapel Hill, NC: The University of North Carolina Press.

Rato, R., & Davey, G. (2012). Quality of life in Macau, China. *Social Indicators Research, 105*(1), 93–108.

Schuessler, K. F., & Fisher, G. A. (1985). Quality of life research and sociology. *Annual Review of Sociology, 11*(129), 39–149.

Selin, H., & Davey, G. (2012). *Happiness across cultures: Views of happiness and quality of life in non-Western cultures.* Dordrecht, The Netherlands: Springer.

Sewell, W. H. (1940). A scale for the measurement of farm family socio-economic status. *The Southwestern Social Science Quarterly, 21*(2), 125–137.

Sirgy, M. J., Michalos, A. C., Ferriss, A. L., Easterlin, R. A., Patrick, D., & Pavot, W. (2006). The quality-of-life (QOL) research movement: Past, present, and future. *Social Indicators Research, 76*(3), 343–466.

Skinner, J. (Ed.). (2012). *The Interview: An ethnographic approach.* London, England: Bloomsbury Academic.

Smith, K. (2002). Some critical observations on the use of the concept of 'ethnicity' in Modood. Ethnic Minorities in Britain. *Sociology, 36*(2), 399–417.

Smith, K., Staples, J., & Rapport, N. (Eds.). (2015). *Extraordinary encounters: Authenticity and the interview.* New York, NY: Berghahn Books.

Stryker, S. (2000). *Symbolic interactionism: A social structural version.* Menlo Park, CA: Benjamin/Cummings Publishing Company.

Veenhoven, R. (2000). Introduction. *Journal of Happiness Studies, 1*(4), 419–421.

Badagas Going Digital

Abstract Claims that new media are fundamentally changing life in India raise interesting questions about how and why people are using them, and their implications, which is the overarching direction of the study described in this chapter. It begins by looking at the paucity of media and visual studies of the Nilgiri Hills and its people, and the role of media as a facilitator of cultural change. Next is an analysis of content in an Internet forum, online portrayals of life and the goings-on of Badagas including their past and current circumstances. Conversations in the forum spanned a wide array of topics relevant to Badagas which have been grouped in the following main themes: Past and present, Pride of being Badaga, Poverty and social inequality in the Nilgiri Hills, and Fundraising and social activism. The chapter also examines positive and negative implications of new media for quality of life, a starting point for an extrapolation to the future. As the first study of their new media use, it reveals important findings and shows they now have an online presence and virtual communities.

Keywords Badagas · Internet forum · New media · Nilgiri Hills
Visual anthropology

Many people today would find it difficult to imagine themselves without an Internet connection, an inseparable part of daily life. Distinctions between online and offline worlds are now less clear as they merge and transform each other. Since the beginning of the ethnography in 2008 there has been an appreciable rise of new media usage among Badagas, especially young people. I regularly interact with Badagas through electronic mail (e-mail), social networking services, and mobile apps. They use the Internet for the same purposes as other people such as access to information, business, communication, entertainment, social networking, and shopping; and numerous personal webpages and blogs have been created by Badagas, insightful information and musings about life supplemented with photos, music, and videos. These changes are located in broader rise of a network society (Barney 2004; Castells 2000).

This chapter is a case study of new media usage and online interaction among Badagas. It examines their lives through an Internet forum, a website with posted messages and conversations, specifically online portrayals of being Badaga and qual-

© The Author(s) 2018
G. Davey, *Quality of Life and Well-Being in an Indian Ethnic Community*,
SpringerBriefs in Well-Being and Quality of Life Research,
https://doi.org/10.1007/978-3-319-90662-1_3

ity of life and the nature of the new type of virtual community, a lens through which to examine Badagas in contemporary India. It begins with a discussion of the paucity of media and visual studies of Badagas, the need for further research, and the role of media as a prime information source and facilitator of cultural change. Next is an analysis of content in an Internet forum created specifically for Badagas. As the first study of its kind among an Indian ethnic minority, it reveals important findings.

There is a paucity of media and visual studies of the Nilgiri Hills. Some visual documentary exists, especially photography. The photographer Albert Thomas Watson Penn (1849–1926) travelled to Ooty at the age of 16, and later set up a photography business and remained there for thirty-years until his death. His work was commissioned for the first editions of Edgar Thurston's *Castes and Tribes of South India* (1909), Frederick Price's *Ootacumund: A History* (1908), and other works. The numerous photographs constitute a significant visual record of the social history of the Nilgiris, as documented in a biography researched and written by his great grandson (Penn 2008). Many photographs of Badagas have also been published in academic works; an excellent example is Hockings's photo essay of funeral practices (2001).

The impact of media on culture and society in India is well documented (Singhal and Rogers 2006). Hockings studied media consumption among Badagas. In 1963, Badagas in four villages were asked questions about their news-gathering habits, and they replied the main sources of news were friends and relatives, newspapers, and officials (Hockings 1999). Radio broadcasting was not a main news source in the 1960s. However, I suspect it would have been in the 1970s onwards, and therefore a key facilitator of change. All India Radio, officially known as Akashvani, the main public radio broadcaster, aired news only twice daily in the 1960s. In the late 1960s onwards, transmitter stations and broadcasting services expanded across the country, and personal ownership of radios increased substantially when relatively cheap sets became available. Consistent with the socialist policies of the Nehruvian era, All India Radio produced education programmes dealing with community development, education, environmental protection, family planning, literacy, and marriage (Singhal and Rogers 2006). The low socio-economic status of Badagas at that time meant they were a likely priority audience for the rural development messages carried by All India Radio (in 1963, for example, 29% of men and 65% of women were illiterate; Hockings 1999). Radio would have also introduced different lifestyles and orientations towards life including aspirations of upward mobility. However, radio programmes tailored to the people in the Nilgiri Hills only became available in 1994 when the Ooty Radio Station, a local radio station of All India Radio, was established to provide local news alongside national programmes (Jayaprakash 2000). In 2013 it began broadcasting a daily news bulletin in Badagu titled 'Seemai Suddhi' (local news) with local presenters, and planned to gradually include other local languages. Prior to the 1990s, then, Badagas only had access to national and regional radio stations.

Television was not available in the Nilgiri Hills at the time of Hockings's study, although his survey respondents reported watching films once or twice a month, especially films which he categorized as mythological and semi-historical melodramas ('traditional dramas' with dancing and singing) and modern social dramas (new comedies, romances, and tragedies). Television was introduced to New Delhi in 1959, and its popularity grew slowly until the 1980s when the launch of Indian satellites and large-scale television transmitters improved broadcasting capabilities (Singhal and Rogers 2006). Badagas probably encountered television in the 1970s and 1980s when there was an expansion of broadcasting and ownership, especially cable and satellite channels with engaging programmes and linguistic plurality. However, initial uptake was slow. For example, Hockings (1999) notes that Kiy Odeyaratti village in 1990 had one television set per 159 people, Oranayi had one per 104, Hullada had one per 57, and Keti Torekeri had one per 49. He also reported differential access to other types of communication: telephones, post offices, telegraph offices, and roads. Television broadcasting was characterised by education and development programmes until the 1990s when it was commercialized, spurred by economic reforms, privatisation of state-controlled media, removal of government regulations, and access to global markets. Doordarshan, the public television broadcaster, and previously the sole provider of television services in India, was joined in the market by a host of foreign and private broadcasters such as MTV, STAR-TV, and Zee-TV. Financed by commercial advertising, they propagated Western values, capitalism, and consumerism through adverts and the lifestyles of actors and actresses. My observations suggest almost every household now has a colour television, partly due to rising living standards and political reasons. Dravida Munnetra Kazhagam (DMK), a political party in Tamil Nadu and Puducherry, won parliamentary elections in 2004 and state assembly elections in 2006, and formed the Government of Tamil Nadu as a coalition with Pattali Makkal Katchi (PMK). The leader of the DMK, acting in his role as Chief Minister of Tamil Nadu, fulfilled his election manifesto promise of a free colour television for every household, and the state government spent about Rs. 1.62 crore (16.2 million). Although the scheme was subsequently suspended by the Election Commission of India, which ruled such gifts an inappropriate influence on votes in favour of the party in power, many Badagas had already received their free televisions.

Up to the 1980s, media in India were primarily print and analog broadcasting (newspapers, radio, and television). In recent times there has been development of digital and new media which many observers consider to be fundamentally changing the ways people live and communicate; a voluminous literature has debated the positive and negative implications (Best and Kellner 2001; Lievrouw and Livingstone 2002; Hiltz and Turoff 1993; Singhal and Rogers 2006). Cyberculture or Internet studies have blossomed since the Internet began to make its presence felt in the 1990s. There is now a huge body of research on technology-mediated communication including classic studies about online identities and virtual communities (Davey 2012; Rheingold 1993; Turkle 1995), cyberculture-related anthologies (Jones 2002), and critical cyberculture studies (Miller and Slater 2000; Silver and Massanari 2006). Research is limited in India, but demand for computers, Internet services, and mobile technology is increasing substantially with technological advances and rising incomes (Singhal and Rogers 2006). In 2017, there were over 462 million Internet users in India (34% of the population), although the proportion of Badagas with Internet access is likely to be lower. No media or visual studies of Badagas have been conducted since Hockings's visit in the 1960s which was only exploratory and preliminary. He intended to replicate his study in the 1990s with the same population and survey questions to identify changes in media usage over one generation but his funding proposal to the National Science Foundation was rejected, and 'we are thus left to guess at how much attitudes may have changed since 1963' (Hockings 1999, p. 232). The paucity of research underscores the need for this chapter, and is a marked contrast to social science generally where Internet research is blossoming (Davey 2008, 2010).

Claims that new media are fundamentally changing life in India raise interesting questions about how and why people are using them, and their implications for identities and quality of life, which is the overarching direction of the study described here. The study is an analysis of conversations in an Internet forum dedicated to Badagas, with focus on portrayals of identities and quality of life: How do Badagas use new media such as the Internet? How are images of being Badaga created and shaped through online platforms? How do these features sculpt a collective persona? And, what are the consequences of new media in terms of identity and quality of life? The not-for-profit Internet forum is ideal for answering these questions as it was created by Badagas for Badagas, and geared to their specific experiences, a unique space for users. It was popular for communication, making connections, and community building. It was also an important source of information about the goings-on of Badagas and their past and current circumstances which permeated almost every post including new material hitherto undocumented. Therefore, the chapter is primarily an analysis of self and life among forum members. It is also a review of debates about identities by people interacting in a space specifically created to attract and support conversations about being Badaga. In other words, the Internet forum provided specialist cultural knowledge pertaining to individual and collective experiences among people who identified as a member of a social category (Badagas), and also the construction of diverse identities within the category as they came together and interacted regardless of what form their affiliation took. The study analyses how identities are played out online, deconstructs strategies of identity work, and theorises their implications, particularly the relevance of claims that new technologies could radically transform self, life, and society (Best and Kellner 2001; Lievrouw and Livingstone 2002; Singhal and Rogers 2006). As noted above, television and radio were probably instrumental in changes among Badagas for much of the twentieth century, but the significance of new media is difficult to evaluate without empirical research. Therefore, the chapter examines their positive and negative implications for quality of life, a starting point for an extrapolation to the future when new media will be more popular among Badagas and could sharpen the ability to resolve life's challenges.

The methodology of the study is detailed in Chapter "Methodology". The Internet forum posts spanned a wide array of topics relevant to Badagas which have been grouped in the following main themes: Past and present, Pride of being Badaga, Poverty and social inequality in the Nilgiri Hills, and Fundraising and social activism. They are discussed below.

Past and Present

There was discussion in the Internet forum about the characteristics and history of the Badaga community in the Nilgiri Hills. Its population size was estimated to be between 250,000 and 350,000 (about 20% of the local population), and the number of hatties to be between 300 and 500. These estimates were based on census data, common knowledge among forum users, and logical reasoning in their posts. For example, one user asked others to post the names of all-known hatties, and they replied with lists of hatties, debates about their completeness, and arguments for and against the addition and deletion of names.

Forum users expressed feelings of resentment and injustice about the unavailability of up-to-date population and socio-demographic data about the community—its economy, people, public services, and social issues. They also criticised the underrepresentation of Badagas in literature and websites. For example, a website created by the Tamil Nadu Government about local ethnic minorities did not mention Badagas, and the Census of India grouped them with other Indians in the 'Kannada, Badaga and Kodagu' sub-group. They felt that Badagas had been treated differently to others in the Nilgiris, and rendered invisible, through official policies. The Government and others were accused of weakening the seperateness of Badagas by neglecting them, and blurring boundaries between them and others, in official records and media reports, interpreted in the forum as a threat to their authenticity and existence. While they acknowledged a social unity of all Indians based on common beliefs and practises, they emphasised the distinctiveness of Badagas based on their community, customs, history, and language, which they reasserted by writing about it and calling for recognition as a separate group in websites and official records. Thus the participants in the forum, under the auspices of being Badaga, came to see a danger or threat posed by the 'other' as jeopardising their identity, importance, and survival, and developed a discourse about protecting their people.

One suggestion to remedy the situation was to collect demographic information about Badagas through initiatives such as compiling: Censuses of residents in the Nilgiri Hills; contact directories with everyone's details; and genealogical trees of residents and their ancestors, descendants, and family relationships, which could be constructed by asking elders to recall family relationships. They also discussed the potential of the Internet to gather information. For example, one forum member introduced his village by creating a page on Wikipedia, an openly editable online encyclopedia, and locating it on Wikimapia, an online map and satellite imaging resource of locations around the world; other forum members subsequently used Wikimapia and posted links and messages to their villages. They also posted links to other types of information about Badagas hosted on other websites such as photo albums and family details.

Another idea they discussed was genetic genealogy of Badagas using DNA testing. Several people reported they had taken DNA tests for genealogy purposes, and they shared the test results in the forum. The tests were Y chromosome (Y-STR) tests for paternal ancestry which analyse DNA samples (a buccal swab of the cheek was mailed to a laboratory for analysis and interpretation in a written report). They have become affordable and available in India, typically marketed to consumers in print and television advertisements. However, forum members struggled to understand the test results as they were lay-people with no training in genetics. For example, one person's test results showed a high frequency of the R1a1 Haplogroup and microsatellite Y-STR variation, which he argued could be a genetic marker of Badagas, an effort to reify a group identity based on biological distinctiveness and hereditary; indeed, many of them perceived Badagas to be a large related family united by genetics and shared descent. Others thought the test results implied relatedness to Coorgs (Kodavas), a community from Kodagu in South India, as they also have the same Y chromosome Haplogroup, or an origin in Europe as a significant number of Europeans also have that genetic marker. A counter argument was the existence of the R1a1 Haplogroup in populations across large areas of Asia and Europe which shows it is not specific to Badagas (indeed, academic studies suggest R1a1a most likely originated in South Asia, and has a high frequency in a number of demographic groups, especially ethnic minorities in South India). In response to speculation of a European origin of Badagas, it was pointed out that all ancestors of the Indian population would have migrated from Europe, known among evolutionary biologists as the African origin of modern humans (Out of Africa hypothesis) which asserts humans originated in Africa and then migrated to the Middle East, Europe, Asia, and the Americas; it was also noted that the concept of a European migration might have been invented by missionaries in colonial times as a strategy to promote religious conversion to Christianity. Contributors to the forum realised the speculative nature of their ideas which did not make any useful contribution to knowledge. They also noted the limited availability of information about genetics of Badagas, and advocated for more research, which positioned the lack of genetic-testing as an identity-based problem. There are obvious problems with suggestions in the forum that there might be fundamental biologically-based divisions between Badagas and others, the idea that there is somehow a distinctive type of Badaga DNA. In short, the definition of an ethnic or social group, whether Badaga or another, is not based on biology and genes, and is never static.

Despite limited genetics research, they were aware of academic studies of Badagas. They thanked several scholars, and called for some kind of honour or recognition to be bestowed on them by the Badaga community. In particular, they singled out Professor Paul Hockings. His books *Counsel from the Ancients: A study of Badaga proverbs, prayers, omens and curses* (Hockings 1988), and *Kindreds of the Earth: Badaga household structure and demography* (Hockings 1999), were deemed to be very important. However, forum members complained they were expensive and, therefore, out-of-reach for many people; some people were restricted to free previews on Google Books, an Internet service that stores extracts of texts in its digital database. They also noted books authored by Badagas, such as *Paamé* written by Balasubramaniam (2009), and the forum was used to promote and invite papers for a new online academic journal about tribal studies founded and edited by a Badaga.

The history of the Badaga community in the Nilgiri Hills was discussed. Forum posts retold a legend about its supposed origins during the reign of Tipu Sultan, the

Muslim ruler of the Kingdom of Mysore. The legend was summarised as follows: A family of seven brothers and a sister lived in a village called Badagahalli in the Talaimalai Hills near Mysore. Tipu Sultan, riding on horseback in the vicinity, was mesmerised by the young woman's beauty, and desired to marry her. Consequently, the family, being staunch Hindus, fled their home during the night, and migrated to the hills where they established the first village. The young woman's disguise of tattooed forearms and forehead, which made her unrecognisable as she fled, subsequently became the distinctive dress and tattoos of Badaga women.

The legend mirrors a popular folk belief among Badagas about the establishment of the community in the Nilgiri Hills by ancient migrants from the former Mysore region in 1500 AD onwards following the break-up of the Kingdom of Vijayanagara, discussed in Chapter "Introduction". Forum users debated the plausibility of the migration, and speculated on the ancestral caste at the time of the Vijayanagara Empire, such as its name, religion, and lifestyle. Suggestions included Kodavas based on perceived cultural similarities with Badagas and the name of their Gram panchayat ('Badaga') in Kodagu district in Karnataka; Lingayats in Karnataka, as they follow the Lingayat custom as well as other similar practices; Badaganadu Balliga community in Karnataka, which originated in north Karnataka and later resettled around Bangalore and Mysore; Mallavalli in Mandya District situated between Mysore and Bangalore, based on similar house designs; Bhoj village in Rajasthan, based on a forum member's family stories; and Punjab in West Bengal, as some Badagu words are also used in the Punjabi language. An alternative argument put forward was that Badagas are indigenous to the Nilgiri Hills, justified with reasons such as the absence of a written Badagu script which could rule out relocation from Mysore and other places with scripted languages; improbability of a small migrant population being able to establish and flourish in the hills; and the high incidence of Sickle Cell Trait among Badagas and other indigenous people, regarded as an evolutionary adaptation among natives.

Small groups of friends and social acquaintances in the Nilgiris and elsewhere have formed Badaga associations which represent the interests of Badagas and promote cultural and social welfare activities. The majority of associations are open to everyone but a minority are private and closed to public membership, and some places have more than one. The oldest is the Young Badaga Association which was formed in 1961 under the Society's Act 1860, and was granted half an acre of land in Ooty by the Government to conduct activities. Other Badaga associations were listed in the forum. Forum members wrote it was difficult to obtain the details of local associations, and not everyone in a city or locality were aware of their existence. The majority of posts were requests for details of specific associations, and replies with the names, addresses, and telephone numbers of the organisers; and representatives of associations also used the forum to advertise their details and events. Forum members also discussed their experiences of attending events organized by the associations. They enjoyed opportunities to meet others, and partake in cultural activities, especially dance and meals; however, they criticized the infrequency of meetings, low attendance by young people, and limited action to improve quality of life, as they tended to be small groups of volunteers with few resources. However, several associations were praised for their social welfare activities, for instance an association in Coimbatore which operated an ambulance service to transport residents from the Nilgiri Hills to hospitals in the city. There were also reports of in-fighting between associations, labelled in the forum as 'political factions'. Suggestions for improvement included the compilation of a list of all associations; collaboration and merger of associations in the same town or city to pool efforts and resources and reduce conflicts; establishment of a physical presence with buildings, offices, and leadership structures for strength and visibility, as existing arrangements were regarded as weak and transitory with low visibility; and provision of education, health, and social welfare services rather than only social activities.

The forum was regarded as a kind of Badaga association or community, and was praised for creating opportunities for people separated geographically and socially to meet and socialise, a place where they could drop in, have a chat, seek or give advice, debate issues, and interact with others, although there were varying levels of personal involvement ranging from fleeting to enduring. It connected Badagas outside the Nilgiris to pursue common interests and purposes, namely information-sharing and social ties. Sociality in the forum centred on posts and responses, many of which developed as chains of social interaction, the glue that held it together in its electronic space. Some contributors appeared to be a committed group of people in close association with each other.

Pride of Being Badaga

A sense of pride and worthiness of being Badaga was portrayed in the dialogues. Badagas were described as dignified, diligent, ethical, generous, hardworking, heroic, honest, hospitable, humble, and intelligent. Forum members revered: traditional lifestyles and customs which emphasised a simple way of living within means, and also family and community; courtesy and hospitality towards strangers and visitors in the Nilgiris; and Hinduism. They were also proud of being born in the Nilgiris.

They wrote about the achievements of Badagas. The development of the community in the Nilgiri Hills—from a small group of migrants to a sizeable population with geographical spread in India and overseas—was regarded as a major accomplishment. The founders of the community were praised for bravery and their folklore which they regarded as inspirational. They also admired folk medicine and village architecture and design such as houses facing east and west to ensure sufficient natural light, locations next to water sources, terraced designs to economise building materials, and drainage systems to prevent flooding. Folklore was also praised for containing scientific facts.

They also shared news of recent achievements by Badagas and themselves. Individuals thought to be of good standing were named in forum posts including academics, agriculturalists, doctors, elders, entrepreneurs, entertainers, government officials, journalists, politicians, and scientists—mostly professionals and experts with specialized knowledge, and people dedicated to serving the community. They listed the names of people believed to be the first Badagas to have achieved a specific status or job. However, doubts were raised about the authenticity of the lists as some names were based on speculation and not official documentation, and some posters questioned whether they were worthy of recognition. Others argued that a handful of success stories did not generalise to Badagas as a whole; indeed, the overly positive characterisations were counterbalanced with examples of cheating, hostility, and misbehaviour (alcoholism, real estate fraud, and a murder case).

There was discussion of artists, entertainers, and people working behind the scenes in the entertainment industry: Actors, singers, musicians, cameramen, directors, producers, and song writers. Musicians and singers had earned a living by performing Badaga music and songs, and producing digital media (and non-digital media like cassette tapes and records). Forum members discussed performers and their music, wrote congratulatory messages, and posted web links to audio recordings and video clips; and producers of music and films posted information about their work. There were also reviews and comments about films portraying Badaga culture and language and other topics with Badaga actors, actresses, and directors. According to forum posts, the first commercialised 'Badaga film' was *Kala Thappitha Payilu* released in the 1980s in the ATC Theatre in Ooty, followed by the film *Kennanju*. The first colour movie was *Hosa Mungaru* produced by MKV Films. People also posted news about theatrical performances and movies in production in the Nilgiris including details and locations of filming, and opportunities to meet in Ooty to watch newly-released movies. Singers and producers had encountered difficulties releasing music and films commercially, and amateur singers had incurred monetary losses because of high production costs, limited sales, and lost profits to pirated copies. However, they regarded performing arts to be an ideal way of imparting knowledge about culture, and called for more Badaga films and music to serve this purpose. Other barriers to careers in entertainment included a lack of support from elders and parents for young people's acting and singing ambitions, and few music or performing arts schools in the Nilgiris. They congratulated entertainers for overcoming these challenges. Another complaint was misrepresentation of Badagu and traditional dance and dress in films. For example, the Tamil movie *Azhage Irrukai Bayamai Irrukkithu* was criticised for its inaccurate portrayal of Badaga culture by non-Badaga actors from Manihatty. It was argued in the forum that only 'genuine' Badaga culture should be shown in movies and in public to protect its authenticity, although others pointed out they should be proud that Badagas had been showcased in media despite misrepresentations, alternative opinions about how they should be portrayed to others.

The forum was used to describe and explain various customs, and to request guidance on their formalities. Examples include Hethai Habba, a festival for worshiping a goddess; Blessing of Elders, a ritual whereby a young person sought blessings of elderly people; wedding and funeral practices; Badaga Day; and traditional dishes and their ingredients, recipes, and preparation. Forum members wrote personal accounts of their experiences in festivals including recent and past events and reminiscence of childhood memories, and they posted links to photos and videos of festivals as well as news about future events in the Nilgiris. For the Badagas writing in the forum, language served as a marker of their group identity.

Badagu was regarded as a distinct language with definitive sounds and words and no script; it was compared to Tamil to demonstrate its exclusivity. They proposed the adaption of English, Kannada or Tamil scripts to reproduce Badagu phonetics, and each was weighed-up in forum posts to identify the most appropriate. However, they were concerned about the apparent declining popularity of Badagu. Many people now communicate in English and Tamil. Some of the forum members wrote they had limited knowledge of Badagu. There were numerous requests for explanations and translations of Badagu names, phrases, proverbs, and songs, to which others responded with answers and commentary on cultural and historical aspects of the language. For example, a forum member recalled a funeral ceremony in the Nilgiri Hills when nobody in a crowd of nearly one thousand knew Karu Harusodhu, a prayer repeated several times before burial or cremation for the soul to be free of all sins. Replies to his post confirmed others also did not know the prayer (and many other sayings), and they expressed feelings of embarrassment and guilt. These concerns were evident in discussions about the declining popularity of Badagu names for boys and girls, and the rising popularity of non-Badagu names. In times past, children were named after their ancestors (usually a deceased grandparent) to remember the dead and differentiate Badagas and others, and also after villages and seemai to identify place of residence. Names of villages were often linked to nature, such as Bikka Mora Hatti (Olive Tree Village), and Hubbathale (Chinese Pagoda Tree Village). In recent times, English and Tamil baby names have become more common. Forum members expressed concern about the declining popularity of traditional naming practices, and argued for their preservation.

This situation was perceived negatively as a failure to connect with their culture and values, and as a threat to the survival of the language which they feared could become extinct. Badagas writing in the forum were anxious about losing the distinctiveness of their group, and emphasised collective responsibility for protecting it through language usage. They suggested that everyone should continue to use and teach Badagu to ensure its popularity and survival, for example adults living in cities and overseas could make an effort to speak and teach it to their children, and retirees could convey their knowledge to younger people. However, others wrote in support of language change which they regarded as unavoidable and also necessary for current circumstances. The utility of Badagu was described as very limited outside the Nilgiri Hills. They argued Badagas should embrace rather than oppose the language shift, for example by improving their competence in English. To counter argue criticism in the forum about children growing up in cities with a limited knowledge of Badagu, they reasoned that migrants have to adapt to new locations, just as their ancestors had done when they migrated to the hills and underwent subsequent cultural adaptation and innovation. They felt proud to belong to a community which embraced change to survive and succeed. It was also pointed out that Badagu has never been static, and is constantly changing; its vocabulary is now a mix of Badagu, English, and Tamil, as numerous words have infiltrated daily conversation. The flexibility of Badagu was evident in posts about proverbs. Forum members listed proverbs along with translations from a book (*Counsel from the Ancients: A study of Badaga proverbs, prayers, omens and curses*; Hockings 1988), and they debated interpretations, and concluded that more than one version of a proverb was possible and modified and interpreted differently by different people and villages. They also noted some people apparently preferred English and Tamil to Badagu, for several reasons. For example, these languages displayed to others they had 'modern lifestyles'; one contributor to the forum even claimed some people pretended they did not understand Badagu as they perceived it to be backward. Young people desired to be fluent in English to secure professional jobs in India and abroad, and they focused on learnig English rather than Badagu, with support of their parents. Badagas with excellent English proficiency living in cities and overseas were regarded as role models and reference groups to which young people aspired.

There were discussions about the legal and political status of Badagas. The Government does not designate Badagas as a Scheduled Tribe, a special title conferred by the Constitution of India to afford economic assistance. As some Badagas want to be a Scheduled Tribe, forum members weighed up the benefits and costs. The benefits they perceived hinged on: Government support to ease quality of life challenges in the Badaga community, especially for people in need of financial support to improve their lives; reserved places in the civil service and higher education; and resources and funding for rural healthcare services and small- and medium-scale enterprises. They also thought it would strengthen an image of Badagas as separate to non-tribals in the Nilgiri, which currently tend to be clubbed together with Badagas by the Government and others. However, forum members also argued against a reclassification. The assumption that Badagas as a whole needed assistance was regarded as absurd—an unfairness of affirmative action. As the wealthiest indigenous group in the Nilgiri Hills, they were not regarded as the neediest of assistance, although others pointed out many people had financial issues and needed help. Also, as a Backward Class, Badagas were already eligible for assistance with economic, educational, and social resources, but only a small number of people had benefited, and thus entitlement to further assistance was questioned. For example, in reply to a forum member's complaint that Badagas in Bangalore were not on a list of Backward Classes entitled to higher education admission quotas, it was counter argued that most students eligible to attend colleges and universities tend to be from elite schools and wealthy families, and therefore less likely to be in need of financial assistance, and that university admission should be merit-based, tied to academic achievement and not caste criteria. It was pointed out that it did not guarantee additional support as pledges by the Government had not always materialised. 'Scheduled Tribe' was regarded as a demeaning tag, indicative of being socially backward, as some people in India look down on the most disadvantaged groups, a reflection of a stigma of government support as well as the caste system in which people are socially-stratified and ranked, a practice which dates to the historical official designation in British India which labelled some tribes as 'criminals' under the Criminal Tribes Act 1871. Some people were concerned that a Scheduled Tribe label would tarnish their reputation and image, and hinder rather than facilitate opportunities. Some complained the move to become a Scheduled Tribe had diverted attention and effort from key issues, and they urged people to instead address problems rather than fight to rely on government handouts, a change in attitude rather than identity. They had already been campaigning for decades, and lacked support of politicians in the regional and national governments. It was also claimed the majority of Badagas were disinterested in the matter. A forum member created an online poll for others to vote for or against becoming a Scheduled Tribe: 53% (26 respondents) voted in favour, 42% disagreed, and 3% were undecided, which shows an ambivalent attitude worthy of research.

Another discussion was about a news story published in *The Hindu* (Radhakrishnan 2007) which reported the inclusion of the Nilgiris in a list of parliamentary constituencies reserved for Scheduled Castes and Scheduled Tribes under the Constitution of India (as the Delimitation Commission allocates seats in parliament for these groups based on their proportion in each state). According to the article, the news had evoked a mixed reaction in the Nilgiris. Scheduled Castes and Scheduled Tribes (Kotas, Kurumbas, Paniyas, and Todas) had welcomed the move, whereas Badagas complained they had been denied representation in parliament. In the article, the Government was accused of politically isolating and marginalising them, and also misunderstanding demographics as they had less weight in politics despite being the numerically-largest ethnic minority community in the Nilgiri Hills (an increasing number of candidates in MP and MLA elections since the late 1980s had been recruited from other castes, unlike in the past when they were only Badagas). Badagas considered the decision to be an injustice, and representatives of Badaga associations had sent letters to the President, Prime Minister, and Chief Minister urging reconsideration. Forum comments about the news story mostly concurred with the views expressed in the story, and blamed politicians for insufficient support. A forum member posted a letter template he had sent to the President of India to urge the Government to reconsider its decision, and requested others to also send it. Identification as Badaga, then, united belief in the right to political control over the Nilgiris.

Poverty and Social Inequality in the Nilgiri Hills

Poverty and social inequality also characterised the forum. Commentary about poverty centred on the demise of the local tea industry since the 1990s, and its negative implications for quality of life. The incomes and living standards of farmers had declined. For example, one post cited a newspaper article published in 2005 that reported the average price of tea was the lowest since the 1990s; and another post quoted an unpublished study by students in SRM University which found 32% of households reported a monthly income of less than Rs. 2000, and only 16% earned over Rs. 10,000. To escape hardship, Badagas had migrated to towns and cities, labelled by forum members as the 'second wave of migration' in recognition of both its magnitude (one estimate put the number of migrants at 8000 families) and the widely-held belief that the Badaga community in the Nilgiri Hills was founded by migrants. They discussed the consequences of rural-to-urban migration. A major concern was the sale of houses, land, and tea estates by Badagas, regarded as a violation of inheritance customs which typically involved passing on property to children. It was claimed some out-migrants had sold their land at absurdly low prices because they did not understand land value, or were desperate for money. Demographic change was described as severe in some villages, as their populations had dwindled—empty houses and a conspicuous absence of people marked the landscape. Also, some people had sold their property and land to non-Badagas who had then settled in the community and brought a different way of life, a stark contrast to several decades ago when apparently only Badagas resided there. Forum members were worried these events might destroy their community in the Nilgiri Hills, and they questioned whether Badagas would continue to exist, a pessimistic outlook for the future. Another concern they discussed was whether the Badaga diaspora would uphold their culture and way of life outside the Nilgiris, and they cited examples of children living in cities (second-generation migrants) with limited knowledge of Badaga customs and Badagu. Some argued for the conditional sale of land and tea gardens whereby buyers and sellers give assurances of future ownership by and employment of Badagas, although others counter argued that doing so was illegal and also unfair as they had bought land and property in many places in India and overseas. Another suggestion was provision of cultural and learning activities—Badagu lessons, trips to the Nilgiri Hills, and get-togethers in the city—to impart knowledge to children and young people. These arguments tended to be against rural-to-urban migration, one-sided and protectionist, even though the majority of contributors to the forum were city residents. The construction of Badagas vis-à-vis the 'other' also had a 'sedentary' bias in terms of Badagas described as tied to the Nilgiri Hills; they made the false assumption of sedentary patterns as the norm. The drawbacks of the migration were not weighed-up with its potential benefits, the most important in this case being a reduction of the proportion of disadvantaged and unemployed people in the Nilgiris, money pumped into the Nilgiri economy via remittances, which presumably improved quality of life, and improved links with outside.

Discussions about social inequality emphasised disparate access to education, healthcare, income, and goods and services; unequal treatment of women; and debate about the need for equal opportunities. Forum members noted a marked divide of economic prosperity and living standards between rural and urban areas in Tamil Nadu whereby Badagas had worse living circumstances than many. They were described as living in poverty with low incomes, debts, unemployment, poor infrastructure, and limited life chances. One complaint was education and schooling. The majority of schools in the Nilgiris were government-owned (free attendance), and concerns were expressed about the quality of their teaching and resources. Students in affluent families benefited from private education renowned for high exam pass rates and university acceptance, whereas children in less well-off families attended government schools and were more likely to have a below-average level of education and not continue to university. Another criticism of local education provision was the presence of unaccredited and unreputable institutions, labelled in the forum as 'diploma mills', and a lack of awareness among students and parents about them. Despite these complaints, they also acknowledged progress over the years in the education of Badagas, regarded as a contributor to their economic and social rise and essential for improving people's lives. Previous generations did not have as many opportunities to attend school whereas school attendance is now compulsory and free for all children up to age fourteen. They were proud of Badagas that had graduated from colleges and universities. However, a minority were not convinced about the merits of the education system which they blamed for problems in the Nilgiri Hills. They argued education did not prepare youth for the real world, and had distracted ambitious and talented people from the pursuit of agricultural and business development; unemployment of graduates was another concern. They believed entrepreneurship by school leavers was more important for growth and innovation in the Nilgiris and its economy than higher education.

There were also complaints in the forum about limited access to healthcare. Although general medicine was readily available through primary and community health centres, advanced medical services such as specialists and diagnostic facilities were limited. Badagas typically had to travel to the city for secondary healthcare. However, barriers to accessing health services in urban areas included medical expenses, which meant some people had sold assets or incurred debts, and limited transportation options for the three-hour journey to the city. Positive comments about health in the Nilgiris emphasised important contributions from a range of non-government organisations such as charitable trusts and voluntary organisations which arranged for medical staff to visit villages, and the natural environment as conducive to good health, especially clean air and drinking water.

Another topic discussed was gender inequity. Respect for women was regarded as a pillar of Badaga culture, a view supported in forum posts with examples of folklore, ballads, festivals, and legends. However, society was characterised by male dominance and subordination of women. Women continue to experience unequal treatment in many aspects of life, and face pressure to conform to socialised gender roles. For example, they are expected to relinquish educational and career goals to marry and be primary caregivers in families at a young age; it was estimated in the forum that 90% of Badaga women made career concessions to accommodate marriage and family needs. Consequently, women are underrepresented in higher education and the workforce, especially in professional and senior roles. Women wrote messages in the forum to express feelings that they could only be successful in a male-dominated society if they were determined, independent, and willing to make sacrifices such as remaining single (they believed it was very difficult for women to pursue an education or career when married). Another issue was age of marriage. A bride was expected to be between ages 19 and 23; older women were deemed by some people to be unsuitable for marriage. An example was given of a potential groom and his family that liked everything about a potential bride except her age as she was older than 24 (she had completed a college degree and work experience). Women felt pressured to marry in their early twenties, and therefore sacrifice career and educational dreams; examples cited in the forum included a young woman who discontinued PhD studies because her neighbours questioned her single status, and students pursuing short-duration education programmes which could be completed more quickly.

Forum members called for more opportunities for women and an egalitarian and inclusive society. Gender inequity was condemned as archaic, not in line with present-day ideas of human rights. They also warned that it could tarnish the reputation of Badagas. Others noted that the standing of women in the Badaga community had improved in recent times, and gave examples of successful women in various careers and professional fields (educators, government officials, journalists, scholars, scientists, and social workers). However, others pointed out those examples of successful women were exceptions rather than representative of the majority. The role of women in villages was said to be changing as they took on positions previously reserved for men, and in some cases they had become the primary breadwinner in households, as men's incomes had reduced. Modifications to traditions had also improved the lives of women, notably the abolition of a dowry (in times past, the bride's family was expected to give jewellery and money to the in-law's household), minimal stigma of divorcees and widows, and *Hengava Nadathodu*, a custom of emotional and moral support to daughters and sisters. However, some customs still hindered gender equity, for example limited participation and entry restrictions for women at the Hethai temples at Beragani and Pedhuva hatties during *Hethai Habba*, based on a social taboo of menstruation which is perceived to be ritually unclean. A nascent women's movement was challenging male dominance in society, as many hatties now have *Magalir Kuzhu*, an organisation which advocates women's rights and welfare. These dialogues show women and men were challenging sexism, and thought they had made progress, but also felt there is still a long way to go to attain gender parity. They realised fairness would be difficult to achieve, and discussed the most appropriate ways to bring it about, for example endorsement from prominent Badagas and Badaga associations. A minority of forum posts written by men defended gender disparaties. They argued it was normative and widespread in India, and not specific to Badagas, and that perfect equality did not exist in any society. They also claimed that women in the Badaga community were better off than in many other places. Some people even blamed women for their disadvantaged status, putting it down to their attitude and lack of determination. For example, in reply to a complaint about a young woman unable to continue university studies because her husband disapproved, a forum member counter argued the woman should have chosen a different husband! Some men wrote in the forum that they thought career women were abnormal, freaks, and misfits, as they regarded marriage and family to be a key structure of Badaga society, applied to assert the notion that a woman defining her existence individually rather than in terms of the family was violating social norms.

There were also clashing views about wedding practices: Arranged marriage (same-caste marriage) versus intercaste marriage and love marriage. Badagas had an arranged marriage system whereby the choice of partner and other marriage arrangements were decided by parents and older family members, and bride and groom had limited say in the matter. However, love marriage, a term used to describe free choice of partner by bride and groom based on mutual affection (with or without parental consent), was reported to be increasing in popularity, especially among urban residents. A lively debate in the forum focused on an advert in the *The Hindu* written by a Badaga woman seeking a marriage partner of any caste. A forum member copied and pasted the advert, and asked others to air their views on intercaste marriage and its implications, a deliberate attempt to incite debate. Some argued for adherence to traditional beliefs and practices—that intercaste marriage was unacceptable and shameful. Their case for upholding same-caste marriage centred on a perceived duty to respect customs which they regarded as a cornerstone of being Badaga, linked to concerns about cultural change taking place, a view that traditions should be upheld to prevent their demise. Other reasons they put forward included the inexperience and emotional immaturity of young people, which they thought justified decision making by parents and elders; and social stigma towards intercaste marriage, for example one forum member wrote that people in his hatti had refused to attend the wedding celebrations of an intercaste marriage. Strong support in the forum for same-caste marriage, in combination with other portrayals of Badagas united by blood ties and genetics, shows that for many people being Badaga is understood as ascribed at birth.

However, other writers in the forum were accepting of intercaste marriage and love marriage. They reasoned marriage customs were changeable over time, and gave examples of the abolition of previous practices (e.g. child marriage, polygamy). It was noted the Hindu Marriage Act 1958 did not prohibit intercaste marriage. Supporters of arranged marriages were criticised for following customs uncritically without thinking about their suitability in the present, and branded as hypocrites because they did not uphold many other Badaga customs. One forum member in an intercaste marriage wrote she appreciated the opportunity to learn about her husband's community and culture and vice versa. Another perspective was that intercaste marriage increased genetic diversity in the Badaga population which could reduce the prevalence of inherited disorders such as Sickle Cell Trait and birth defects among children of first-cousin marriages. Customary marriage rules for cross-cousin marriage and reciprocal bride-exchange between hamlets were regarded as confusing and complicated, as young people and their families were unsure about eligibility according to kinship rules, which had encouraged some to seek non-Badaga partners. The customs were also considered to be time-consuming and restrictive, and communicating directly with potential partners rather than through intermediaries was easier. Also, people had additional expectations of potential partners which took priority over customary marriage rules, for example social and financial status; it was claimed that urban residents with good jobs found partners more easily than rural folk. Arranged marriage was criticised for forcing women to follow unjust rules which only served the preferences and interests of the groom and family, and increased the likelihood of a mismatch of bride and groom, with negative consequences for their wellbeing; a case was made to abolish arranged marriage practices to assert women's rights. Other forum members sought a middle ground in the debate by reasoning that intercaste marriage and love marriage were acceptable in certain circumstances, for instance divorcees and overseas residents who encountered difficulties finding Badaga partners, although both sides in the debate could have done more to establish some middle ground.

A more positive interpretation of life in the Nilgiris was also portrayed, albeit in a minority of posts. In some respects, quality of life had improved over time. Most homes were deemed to be comfortable, and each hatty took care of its residents through an informal social security. Also, some people had professional jobs and high salaries. Badagas were placed above the bottom rung of India's poor, as conditions in their villages were said to be better than many other places in rural India and overseas. For example, one forum member compared the quality of life of Badagas to places he had travelled in India, South Asia, and the Far East, and claimed they enjoyed a better standard of living. Life in the Badaga community was weighed up with challenging conditions and stress in cities: competition in society, environmental issues (overcrowding, pollution), and materialism. However, others pointed out that many villages had residents struggling to make ends meet, and some homes had no toilets and water and were in need of improvement. There was commentary on inequalities within and between villages: income and wealth differences, wide gaps between rich and poor, which ranged from people in poverty with limited amenities to wealthy owners of luxury consumer products; in-between these extremes people lived in a range of circumstances. Another complaint was discrimination as some people looked down on others, for example residents in towns and cities had a derogatory attitude towards rural folk, and professionals in Information Technology in Bangalore regarded themselves as superior to people working in less prestigious occupations and companies, the basis of status identities.

Fundraising and Social Activism

As well as trending topics, forum members also worked together to improve quality of life in the Nilgiris. They brainstormed ideas, and took action to implement them. One example was charity fundraising on behalf of a social service organisation. A request was posted for monetary donations to fund medical treatment for a young man with a health condition. The forum was used to introduce the man's condition; arrange a meeting with his family; discuss treatment and hospital options; appeal for forum users and Badaga associations to transfer donations to a specific bank account number; plan and coordinate receipt of donations; and provide updates of the fundraising. People posted messages with details of their donations. The donors were Badagas in cities such as Bangalore, Coimbatore, and Chennai, and also overseas (Dubai Badaga Association). More than 100,000 Rupees was raised, although the proportion donated only by forum users was unclear. The fundraisers conveyed appreciation on behalf of the young man, and the donors and others expressed gratitude and pride. The forum also facilitated the arrangement of 'eye camps', free eye examinations and operations by outreach services of charities and hospitals. For example, an event was held in Jagathala village by the NandiSeva Trust in association with the Shankara Eye Foundation in Kovai and Rotary Club of Ketti Valley. It was used to arrange and advertise the event, and provide an update on its outcome. Posts in the forum reported that 82 people had taken eye tests, and four had surgery. Other charity and social welfare activities arranged in the forum included: A cancer awareness and screening programme; fundraising for elderly people with chronic kidney disease; charity work by Badaga associations; donation of items; and offers of financial sponsorship for people in need.

Forum members gave suggestions to improve the quality of life of Badagas. These included: provision of educational resources (scholarships and monetary prizes for high-performing students, careers advice, and creation of degree courses about agriculture and vocational skills training); agricultural development initiatives (diversification and agricultural co-operatives); financial and technical support for farmers to upgrade inefficient and outdated agricultural methods (forum members gave examples of unprofitable farms sold by Badagas which subsequently became successful under new management); and economic and infrastructure improvement in villages. They also argued for lobbying politicians to take action to improve the Badaga community; arranging for Badagas with expertise and skills (e.g. architects, builders, lawyers, financial advisors and retired government employees) to share their knowledge with others; construction of Badaga-specific institutions and facilities (e.g. a Badaga hotel, hospital, medical camp, school, and public health initiatives); and a proposal to create a charitable trust to lead community development.

A face-to-face meeting of forum members was organised to discuss these ideas. The date and location of the meeting (Ootacamund, 13th August 2006) was arranged in the forum, and five people attended for 3 h in duration. An outcome of the meeting was agreement to create a charitable trust. Subsequent posts in the forum centred on the next steps including tax exemption and legal registration, creation of a business plan and mission and vision statements, opening a bank account, appointment of a management team, and long-term goals such as establishing an educational institution, health centre, and organic farm. A forum member prepared legal deeds for the trust, and posted them online. However, these goals were not accomplished. At the end of 2006 onwards, the activism lost momentum. Several years later the inaction was questioned. Reasons given for failure to follow up the ideas included disinterest, concerns about safekeeping of monetary donations and funds, residence outside the Nilgiris, limited manpower to do groundwork, lack of consensus on projects, and uncertainty about the legality of creating and operating a charitable trust. They also questioned whether the creation of a new trust was necessary as others already existed.

They insisted the Government should initiate measures such as agricultural development, bank loans, infrastructure improvement, and tourism promotion to jump-start the local economy. They criticised politicians and the Tea Board for failing to remedy problems in the tea industry, as solutions had still not been found. Government assistance for farmers was limited in availability and scope. A prevailing opinion in forum posts was a neglect of farmers. They also described barriers faced by farmers trying to access assistance: complex and bureaucratic procedures and stringent conditions which excluded many from eligibility. As well as a failure to solve problems in the agricultural sector, politicians were criticised for other issues such as corruption, favouritism towards the interests of upper and middle classes, and unfulfilled election promises. They were described as dishonest, incompetent, and inexperienced. Forum users were also annoyed about political campaigns in the Nilgiris to influence the decision-making of voters, popular but relatively unimportant election promises (e.g. donating free colour televisions to households). They also discussed strategies to coax politicians to take action. One suggestion was to conduct regular evaluations of their performance by scoring it against attributes and objectives, similar to the United Progressive Alliance's (UPA) *Report to the People*, a report card published every year by the Government which lists its accountability for governance. Another suggestion was tactical voting strategies whereby the Badaga electorate could scrutinise candidates for government positions based on their commitment to the community, or elect only Badaga candidates for Members of Parliament (MP) and Members of the Legislative Assembly (MLA). Forum members discussed details of Badaga politicians including their names, backgrounds, projects, and achievements and failures while in office. Considering the size of the population (35% of the electorate in the Nilgiris, according to one post), they regarded Badagas as a political force which could influence election outcomes. However, others argued that venting blame and frustration at convenient targets like politicians was not a substitute for dealing with the realities of life. These examples of identity politics—political mobilization around identity—reveal that being Badaga was seen as a potential tool and strategy of mobilisation in India's electoral democracy, a form of collective action to influence state politics relating to social justice; when Badagas cast a vote, they vote their caste. Similar to other expressions of protest in the forum, it also highlights the salience of a coherent Badaga identity in expressing discontent and solutions.

The forum was used as a platform for activism to bring about social and economic improvement, the first documented case of Internet activism by Badagas. The activism hinged on forum members' suspicions of unethical business practices in the tea industry. They regarded farmers to be vulnerable and exploited with inadequate compensation for their work. To justify their suspicions of exploitation, forum members summarised the business chain of tea production in the Nilgiris, channels through which it moved from farmers through markets and buyers to consumers. At the beginning of the chain were farmers that grew and harvested tea, mostly smallholders although a few owned bigger estates. They sold tea leaves to agents or collectors which then sold them to tea factories (tea manufacturers). Factories processed tea leaves into ready-to-drink tea which was sold to buyers through intermediaries (auction centres, brokers) in Coimbatore and Coonoor. Tea buyers represented national and international tea companies which had blending, packaging, and trading facilities and sold the final product to retailers and consumers. According to forum posts, the livelihoods of farmers were at the mercy of auction centres and brokers which: controlled the price of tea leaves after tasting and grading and considering market trends; permitted buyers and suppliers to purchase and sell tea; and controlled money flow, as they authorised payments to farmers after deduction of commission and charges. In contrast, the farmers played a more passive role as they did not directly sell products or negotiate prices. Allegations were made in the forum about an illegal cartel of price-fixing among brokers which manipulated prices and buyer and broker availability, resulting in low incomes of farmers. They also claimed some tea factories were debtors to brokers, and owed as much as several lakhs of Rupees because they had borrowed money with high interest rates such as 36% per annum. One example posted was a factory which had borrowed 15 lakhs but later owed 60 lakhs with accrued interest; apparently, 100 factories had closed as a result of inability to repay loans. It was claimed that factories owing money to brokers were less able to negotiate higher prices or seek alternative brokers and buyers, which forum members described as 'bonded labour'. Also, they accused the Tea Board of ignoring the situation. These problems were blamed for the low incomes and quality of life among farmers.

Forum members raised awareness of their beliefs about unethical money lending by brokers to factories and the existence of illegal price-fixing cartels. Forum users requested information from the Tea Board about money lending, in accordance with The Right to Information Act 2005 which obligates public authorities in India to retain and publish records, and permits citizens to request the information. An applicant could expect to receive a reply to their enquiry within thirty days, and was required to pay fees to file requests (Rs. 10), receive information (Rs. 2 per page), and inspect information at record offices (Rs. 5/h). Specifically, information requested from the Tea Board concerned: Rules and records of money lending; action it had taken against its employees for failure to tackle illegal money lending; financial records of all tea brokers in the Nilgiris; and other agricultural issues such as the Tea Quality Upgradation and Product Diversification Scheme, based on forum members' suspicions of corruption and financial irregularities. They also lodged First Information Reports about the suspected money lending (written documents prepared by the police when they first receive information about a crime, to set in motion the criminal justice process with a police investigation), based on the *Tamil Nadu Prohibition of Charging Exorbitant Interest Act 2003* which prohibited unreasonable interest rates on loans.

The activists posted details of their activities, and instructions and templates to assist others to join the activism. Details they posted included reference numbers of information requests, names of brokers presumed to be involved in unethical money lending, and names and addresses of police stations where they had lodged First Information Reports; later forum posts gave updates on the progress of these efforts. Replies they received from the Tea Board, copied and pasted in the forum, confirmed money-lending by brokers to factories and estates was prohibited. The confirmation by the Tea Board was interpreted by forum members as a successful outcome of their efforts which they reasoned paved the way to obtain documentary evidence of money-lending, request cancellation of brokers' licences, and take court action. They also believed their activism had put pressure on the authorities to investigate and remedy the issues they had raised, as they had heard anecdotal reports about increases in tea prices and the ending of advance payments by brokers, which they regarded as a success of their activism (although these claims were neither evaluated nor substantiated). However, the Tea Board stated it was unaware of money-lending in the Nilgiris, and had not received any complaints from factories about brokers charging exorbitant interest rates.

In summary, then, the activism was essentially an online collaboration to advocate farmers' rights and standard of living based on perceptions of an unjust system in which they were mistreated. The activism clearly shows that identity was a resource strategically deployed online, as being Badaga came to the fore when people diagnosed and addressed issues, recognised their group's suffering, and accused those they thought were responsible for the problems, boundaries between them as a collective and others. However, the scope of the activism was limited. Only a minority of forum members participated while the majority only read or commented on posts and did not engage beyond discussion. A search of the Internet reveals the online activism took place only in the forum, in other words only among Badagas in that particular online space, as there was no cross-posting of messages in other outlets (which would have increased awareness of the activism and its cause to a much larger audience). The activism was a small group effort on which a minority of people pinned hopes, and not a social movement that made any real difference. Also, it had a short life-cycle as interest and action gradually declined and waned. Even so, the activists had big ambitions. They suggested collective action by mobilizing Badagas in villages and cities, as they thought a mass movement was needed to turn the tables around for the community in the Nilgiris; several people volunteered to visit hatties to raise awareness of the issues and encourage people to protest.

Forum members complained the activism was burdensome and time-consuming. They experienced hostility and slow replies to their enquiries from public authorities, which they situated in the inefficiency and slowness of the Indian judicial system; for example, a forum member received a reply from a local government office which requested a large photocopying fee (Rs. 238,800) and additional costs to provide the information. Some activists did not understand their replies because they had limited legal knowledge and skills. For example, in a discussion of the *Norms for Licensing of Brokers in Public Tea Auctions* and other rules, which according to forum posts forbid brokers to lend money but permitted advance payment if requested by a factory (with any interest accrued on the advance governed by local laws), they queried legal definitions of advance payment, borrowing, and lending, but did not reach a consensus. Several people reported they had met factory owners to raise awareness and encourage them to file complaints with the Tea Board and police, but they were reluctant to do so as they depended on brokers for business. It was claimed that several factory owners had filed First Information Reports but they were interpreted by others as cunning attempts to default on advance payments, and the police were reluctant to accept them; and brokers, as powerful stakeholders in the tea industry, were accused of delaying the investigations of these cases. Forum members posted mostly supportive messages about the activism, but some questioned the allegations of predatory lending by brokers which had not been verified with evidence. They reasoned money lending was a common business practice, and tea prices were determined by an array of other factors including quality, mismanagement of factories, and inefficient farming methods, which the activism did not target. Concerns were expressed about the quality of tea produced in the Nilgiris which had apparently hampered its reputation, popularity, and market value. Some contributors mentioned media reports which described it as substandard, coarse, and low-grade. However, forum members argued these reports were exceptions and sensational journalism, and not representative of Nilgiris tea as a whole. The activism also did not target other quality of life issues in the Nilgiris. However, the criticism of the activism did not outstrip it, and there was no counter mobilisation in opposition to the activism.

The forum was also used to report news about activism by Badagas in the Nilgiris and nearby areas. One example was a demonstration by hundreds of people protesting the construction of a church in B. Manihatty Village which they claimed threatened the unity of the village, and denigrated their culture (The Hindu 2012; Radhakrishnan 2012). The demonstration took place at the Office of the District Collector (District Magistrate) responsible for the implementation of government programmes in the Nilgiris. Representatives of the villagers held talks with the District Revenue Officer and the Deputy Superintendent of Police. Several people condemned the arrest of eighteen protestors following a row with the villagers who proposed the establishment of the church, demanded the unconditional release of the arrestees, and sought assurance that churches and religious propaganda would not be permitted in the Badaga community. Forum members supported the activists, concurred that the construction of the church would have negatively affected Badaga culture and community, and referred to the proposers of the church as 'traitors' and 'parasites'.

Concluding Summary

In this chapter I explored an online community and its portrayals of quality of life and identities, a lens through which to examine Badagas in contemporary India. A new type of social collective of Badagas, a virtual community connected by online social interaction and notions of culture, is documented. As the first study of their new media usage, it revealed important findings.

The online discussions spanned a wide array of topics, and were a valuable source of information about their lives. Unfortunately, a negative quality of life in the Nilgiri Hills was a salient theme which centred on the demise and low profitability of agriculture. The livelihoods of farmers were characterised as low incomes, debts, unemployment, limited opportunities, and out-migration to nearby cities. There was emphasis in the forum on farmers' vulnerable position in the tea industry whereby the overwhelming proportion of economic returns flowed to other stakeholders, namely middlemen and large tea corporations. Other aspects of low life quality included education, healthcare, infrastructure, and socio-economic inequality. The unfortunate reality was an appreciable number of people struggling for satisfactory living resources. However, the forum was utilised as a tool to improve quality of life. It empowered people to form alliances and work together across geographical boundaries to raise awareness of issues, propose and discuss solutions, and coordinate and take action including e-activism and e-philanthropy. These findings reveal a novel form of collaboration by Badagas, not documented previously, which changed the nature of their advocacy and protesting. Whereas the literature emphasises objective life quality, especially economy and standard of living, based on determinism and macro-level institutions and social structures, this chapter considered subjective quality of life, people's own interpretations of their circumstances.

A strong sense of being Badaga was revealed in forum dialogues, and people articulated different perspectives. As Badagas, they regarded themselves to be distinct with a shared sense of community, customs, ethnicity, history, and language, a collective identification separating them and others, although there was disagreement on the specifics. They wrote about their perceptions of distinctiveness with a sense of pride and worthiness; called for recognition of Badagas as a separate group in websites and official records; and accused the Government and others of neglecting and blurring the boundaries between them and others. Forum members also regarded Badagas to be a distinct group on the basis of blood ties and genetics, which shows that for many people it was understood as ascribed and biological rather than socially constructed. Identity was also brought to the fore in forum discussions about the legal and political status of Badagas, and in collective action to influence state politics relating to inequities and redistribution of resources, the notion that being Badaga was a potential tool and strategy of mobilisation in India's electoral democracy. It was deployed strategically in activism concerning low tea prices and life quality when forum members positioned Badagas as victims, which solidified the 'other' against which they became relevant, and then they worked together to bring about changes when the 'other' posed a threat to their group's circumstances and existence. Badaga solidarity in the forum also served as a rallying point against being 'othered' in the local government and tea industry. Taken together, forum members constructed boundaries to mark their territory—who was a Badaga and who was not—and took action to showcase these perceived differences. Overall, the forum was identity-promoting in the sense it fostered allegiances among Badagas, legitimised the group, and showcased them to the world via the website which was accessible to anyone with an Internet connection.

A look beneath the surface of forum dialogues revealed abstractness and diversity, as many forms of Badaga identities were portrayed which reflected the heterogeneity of backgrounds, lifestyles and views among forum members. This was evident, for example, in lively debates about different images of being Badaga, sometimes characterised by strong sentiments on issues which were contested, defended, and negotiated. Discussions largely revolved around the issue of authenticity—who was a 'real' Badaga and who was not. However, authenticity itself was not clear-cut, and largely hinged on notions of upholding traditions and values among those who wanted to set narrow parameters versus other forum participants who challenged prevailing discourses with alternative perspectives and biographies on which they affiliated with the forum, substantial disagreement about what constituted being Badaga. Also, it was not clear what 'traditional' meant, a vision of the past constructed differently by different forum members. In other words, the forum was a meeting space for people who had very different views and yet identified as Badaga, a medium that facilitated conversations between those who supported traditions and those who refused to self-identify in such terms, a dynamic tension among its diverse members that simultaneously reified for some and diversified for others socially constructed notions of being Badaga. The forum could not be dominated by any particular point of view, as there was no restriction or control of people's voices, unlike in the real world (as documented in the next chapter, which reveals Badagas in Bangalore carefully balanced conformity to competing Badaga identities). Individuals laying claim to particular definitions found that others challenged those claims, and it was this context in which new identities developed from the constant ebb and flow of interactions between people as sites of contestation. Collectively, these findings reveal a diversity of identities and identity-related processes, and the porousness of perceived boundaries with little or no restrictions on the types of images of being Badaga that could be portrayed. However, despite these differences, none of the forum members rejected the Badaga label; indeed, everyone embraced it and expressed pride doing so.

The study's strength is focus on people's experiences and ideas which enables the reader to 'get inside' the minds of Badagas to see the world as they perceive it, revealing diversity and disagreement about quality of life and the cultural markers and boundaries of being Badaga. The symbolic interactionist approach shows identities and ways of living are thoroughly in flux, and contested and negotiated across multiple spaces. The notion of an online Badaga community is also a starting point to dispel the classic representation in the literature of Badagas as a homogenous, spatially-bound, and static caste of more than 160,000 people in the Nilgiri Hills. It challenges reified categories such as 'Badagas' and 'Badaga community' and assumptions that people and culture are local and bounded; in reality, Badagas are multiply situated and moving around India and electronic spaces, an interlinking of identities and circumstances which show they can no longer be understood by sole focus on the Nilgiri Hills. It is important to note the online community was markedly different to the real-world Badaga community, an alternative sociality which challenges previous studies of its culture and society.

The virtual community was not geographically circumscribed but a differentiated form of social space glued together by new media-based social interaction; indeed, most forum members resided outside the Nilgiri Hills without physical propinquity, and the online and offline overlapped and interacted. Time also had different connotations as forum interaction took place over days, weeks, months, and even years, asynchronous and time-lagged. Furthermore, the online community appears to be a type of gift economy whereby information exchange in forum posts took place with expectations of reciprocity (replies from others) and new social connections, an economy which contrasts markedly to the agricultural and manual labour system in the Nilgiris, although the literature documents the existence of a gift economy prior to the 1930s based on interdependent social exchange of products and services. These unique features of an online Badaga community support the conclusions of variation and fluidity of sociality, and offer intriguing opportunities for future research. While advances in media research are obviously not new to social scientists, 'nilgiriologists' have been slow to realize their potential. Yet it is clear that Badagas can no longer be understood without consideration of such current forces, a rethink of ways to study their culture and society.

However, the study was exploratory. The researcher had no control over the key issues addressed in forum posts, as the study was an analysis of archival (secondary) data. The next chapter builds on these findings with a study conducted in the real world with rural-to-urban migrants in Bangalore. It begins with a review of migration in India, especially among Badagas, and then analyses interviews conducted with migrants. Chapter "Migrants' Voices" offers rich information which helps to tease out how they responded to the upheaval of leaving the Nilgiri Hills and living in the city. It also explores further their quality of life in the city, and its intersection with being Badaga, processes of identity change, and criteria by which they constructed distinctions between themselves and others. The second study, then, paints a comprehensive picture of what it means to be a member of their caste in urban areas. The combination of the two empirical studies in the multi-sited ethnography informs a critical conceptualisation of their living circumstances and identities in the final chapter.

References

Balasubramaniam, B. (2009). *Paamé: The history and culture of the Badagas of the Nilgiris*. Bangalore, India: Elkon Animations.
Barney, D. (2004). *The network society*. Cambridge, England: Polity Press.
Best, S., & Kellner, D. (2001). *The postmodern adventure: Science, technology, and cultural studies at the third millennium*. New York, NY: Guilford Press.
Castells, M. (2000). *The Rise of the network society*. Oxford, England: Blackwell Publishers.
Davey, G. (2008). Twenty years of visual anthropology. *Visual Anthropology, 21*(3), 189–201.
Davey, G. (2010). Visual anthropology: Strengths, weaknesses, opportunities, threats. *Visual Anthropology, 23*(4), 344–352.
Davey, G. (2012). Internet. In A. Stanton., E. Ramsamy., P. Seybolt., & C. Elliott (Eds.), *Cultural sociology of the Middle East, Asia, & Africa: An encyclopedia* (pp. IV228–IV230). Thousand Oaks, CA: SAGE Publications.
Hiltz, S. R., & Turoff, M. (1993). *The network nation: Human communication via computer*. Cambridge, MA: The MIT Press.
Hockings, P. (1988). *Counsel from the ancients: A study of Badaga proverbs, prayers, omens and curses*. Berlin, Germany: Mouton de Gruyter.
Hockings, P. (1999). *Kindreds of the earth: Badaga household structure and demography*. New Delhi, India: SAGE Publications.
Hockings, P. (2001). Mortuary ritual of the Badagas of Southern India. *Fieldiana: Anthropology New Series, 32*, 1–72.
Jayaprakash, Y. T. (2000). Remote audiences beyond 2000: Radio, everyday life, and development in South India. *International Journal of Cultural Studies, 3*(2), 227–239.
Jones, S. G. (2002). *Virtual culture: Identity & communication in cybersociety*. London, England: SAGE Publications.
Lievrouw, L. A., & Livingstone, S. (Eds.). (2002). *Handbook of new media: Social shaping and consequences of ICTs*. London, England: SAGE Publications.
Miller, D., & Slater, D. (2000). *The Internet: An ethnographic approach*. Oxford, England: Berg.
Penn, C. (2008). *In pursuit of the past: The discovery of the life and work of A. T. W. Penn, pioneering photographer of South India*. Worplesdon, England: Christopher Penn.
Price, F. (1908). *Ootacamund: A history. Compiled for the Government of Madras*. Madras, India: The Superintendent, Government Press.
Radhakrishnan, D. (2007). Move to make Nilgiris reserved segment evokes mixed reaction. *The Hindu*. Retrieved from http://www.thehindu.com/todays-paper/tp-national/tp-tamilnadu/Move-to-make-Nilgiris-reserved-segment-evokes-mixed-reaction/article14816593.ece
Radhakrishnan, D. (2012). Opposition to church: Protest against arrest of villagers. *The Hindu*. Retrieved from http://www.thehindu.com/news/cities/Coimbatore/opposition-to-church-protest-against-arrest-of-villagers/article2783263.ece
Rheingold, H. (1993). *The virtual community: Homesteading on the electronic frontier*. Reading, MA: Addison-Wesley.

Silver, D., & Massanari, A. (Eds.). (2006). *Critical cyberculture studies*. New York, NY: New York University Press.

Singhal, A., & Rogers, E. M. (2006). *India's communication revolution: From bullock carts to cyber marts*. New Delhi, India: SAGE Publications.

The Hindu. (2012, January 7). Villagers near Udhagamandalam oppose construction of church. *The Hindu*. Retrieved from http://www.thehindu.com/news/cities/Coimbatore/villagers-near-udhagamandalam-oppose-construction-of-church/article2713964.ece

Thurston, E., & Rangachari, K. (1909). *Castes and tribes of Southern India*. Madras, India: Government Press.

Turkle, S. (1995). *Life on the screen. Identity in the age of the Internet*. New York, NY: Touchstone.

Migrants' Voices

Abstract Migration is a positive global phenomenon in scale, complexity, and impact. This chapter is about rural-to-urban migration among Badagas. It begins with a brief review of migration as a salient theme in previous writings about the people, and then describes a study of rural-to-urban migrants in Bangalore to understand more about their experiences of leaving the Nilgiris, living in the city, being Badaga, and becoming City Badaga. It unpacks the complexity of the migrants' lives as they attempted to uphold some sense of autonomy and heritage as Badaga while also becoming functional members of an urban society and searching for a better future. A thread tying together the findings was a deep personal sense of being Badaga, and on this common background rested diversity and flexibility as the chapter shows various ways Badaga identities and quality of life change following migration. The chapter also uncovers the conditions, processes, and contexts of identity construction, and sheds light on complex relationships between migration, identities, and quality of life. It is an important endeavour considering that India has a large number of migrants and urban dwellers and will continue to do so.

Keywords Badagas · Bangalore · Identity · Nilgiri Hills
Rural-to-urban migration · Quality of life

Sensationalist images and stories of people abandoning their homelands, travelling across countries, and living in refugee camps appear regularly in newspaper headlines and on television and electronic screens, an unrelenting stream of reporting which has put migration in the public consciousness. India, the world's second most populous country, has diverse and interesting migration histories, and there is now a vast diaspora spread across every continent. Rural-to-urban migration is a defining feature of the twenty-first century, and has consistently drawn attention. It has resulted in the growth of cities such as Bangalore, Kolkata, Mumbai, and New Delhi, part of a national and global phenomenon as half of the world's population live in urban areas. One-third of the Indian population are now migrants, and about half of them are rural-to-urban migrants—around 100 million people. As demographic change continues, India is likely to have a majority of urban residents in the future.

© The Author(s) 2018
G. Davey, *Quality of Life and Well-Being in an Indian Ethnic Community*,
SpringerBriefs in Well-Being and Quality of Life Research,
https://doi.org/10.1007/978-3-319-90662-1_4

Badagas are also on the move. A prominent topic in Chapter "Badagas Going Digital" was the increasing number of people taking migration journeys to seek a better life in towns and cities, fuelled by disparities in life quality between rural and urban areas—a wave of the urbanisation sweeping across India. There is only a brief mention (Hockings 1999, 2013) of rural-to-urban migration and the growth of non-agricultural employment among Badagas. Thus far, little has been said about the migrants such as who they are and how they live; and there have been no studies of Badagas outside the Nilgiris or in urban areas. Migration is not simply about headlines, numbers, and social economics, but about people's experiences and interpretations. Migration is a personal and social process as well as a demographic and economic one. As little is known about Badagas moving to and living in urban areas, research is needed to explore their rural-to-urban migration experiences. Therefore, this chapter contributes to this gap in knowledge, and gains an appreciation of the ways they make sense of their changing circumstances in relation to being Badaga and life quality. It begins with a brief review of migration and the Nilgiris, followed by an analysis of empirical evidence using primary data from rural-to-urban migrants in Bangalore.

Migration is a prominent theme in writings on Badagas. As discussed earlier, their oral tradition describes successive waves of migration in the sixteenth or seventeenth century by the Vokkaligas (presumed to be the ancestors of Badagas; Hockings 1980), from the southern plains of the former Mysore region, and the subsequent founding of the Badaga community in the Nilgiri Hills. Authors have published detailed analyses of the folk stories including accounts of people presumably escaping war and persecution (Belli Gowder 1923–1941, 1938–1941; Benbow 1930; Emeneau 1944–1946; Hockings 1980, 1999). For this reason, Badagas have been styled as 'refugees' (Hockings 1980). It is thought the first arrivals established several homesteads in the Nilgiri Hills, as shown in Ferreira's record of 500 Badagas in three villages in 1603 which has been described as a recently-established settlement (Ferreira 1603; Hockings 1980). However, as I point out in Chapter "Introduction", the migration proposition remains hypothetical as there is insufficient evidence. Also, the migration has been regarded as a one-way movement in previous studies, as there is no information about the exchanges and links between origin and destination which presumably would have continued. Importantly, there is no information about identity change, for example from Vokkaliga to Badaga. The lack of information could be interpreted to mean the migration did not take place, despite the persistence of a migrant or refugee identity in the literature, as the migration has been taken for granted by scholars without any real critical thinking about its validity. The analysis of Internet forum posts in the previous chapter shows some Badagas challenge the migration hypothesis, and posit an alternative proposition of indigeneity which highlights a need to explore nuances in people's views. It is perhaps surprising that identity change during the supposed establishment of the Badaga community by migrants has not been investigated. That migrants created, and identified as, a new group upon settling in the Nilgiri Hills shows identities were highly fluid and adaptable, and capable of absorbing different cultures and outsiders easily, inclusive rather than exclusive. According to folklore, on reaching the hills the women wore facial tattoos and dressed in white clothes to resemble Kota women, while the men wore Toda shawls for warmth and to resemble them (Benbow 1930; Karl 1945; Hockings 1980). As Hockings (1999, p. 29) notes "they represent perhaps the only well-documented case in Southern Asia of a former caste group adopting a tribal social model for emulation, since usually cultural change has been in an opposite direction: Tribes there emulate and sometimes enter caste society".

There have also been studies of labour migration to the Nilgiris from neighbouring districts and provinces in Tamil Nadu such as Coimbatore, Malabar, and Mysore, when the expanding economy in British India created employment opportunities (Heidemann 1997). The migrants took up all kinds of jobs, as did Badagas and other local people. Examples reported in the literature include labourers in coffee and tea plantations, construction (buildings, roads, and telecommunications), domestic and other workers, and petty traders of merchandise (Heidemann 1997; Hockings 1999; Richards 1932; Zagarell 1997). A notable study is Heidemann's (1997) analysis of migrant labourers in the Nilgiris including the demographic, economic, and social changes following their arrival. They became a significant proportion of the population, and the backbone of the economy. These influences on Badagas have been speculated. For example, the introduction of new ideas and relationships are thought to have replaced former gift and commodity exchanges (Heidemann 1997; Mandelbaum 1955, 1989). It also seems likely that the influx of people led to a more pluralistic society in which the concept of identity, especially for minority and indigenous people, became more important. However, the impact of colonialism on migration and society in the Nilgiris, a reoccurring theme in the literature, has been overemphasised by previous writers. There has been a tendency to divide the history of the Nilgiris into three periods (early, colonial, and post-Independence; Hockings 1999; Mandelbaum 1989) which puts British India at centre stage. It seems to be based on biased assumptions by writers that colonialism was a time of development and success, and superior to the past, even though the economy of India was stagnant under the British Raj and did not undergo industrialisation in the nineteenth century in the way that Britain did. The economic impact of British imperialism on India remains a contentious issue among historians, and is probably not as bright as the picture painted in writings concerning Badagas.

Academic discourse on Badagas and the Nilgiri Hills also aligns with a sedentary bias in anthropological thinking of static, ageless village societies and social structures apparently broken up during the nineteenth century, an old colonial notion of an immobile rural Indian population. The authorities in the colonial period often portrayed the population as fixed and immobile to argue for enhanced mobility. Thus much of the literature makes the false assumption of sedentary patterns among Badagas and others as the norm, and portrays population movement as an exclusively modern phenomenon, although some authors wrote the Nilgiri Hills and bordering areas had extensive and long-term relationships throughout history including migration (Richards 1932), and were integrated into the mainstream (Zagarell 1997). Much historical research in other locations shows that most of the Indian rural population was highly mobile, as population movement was the rule rather than exception. It seems likely that people in the Nilgiris were engaged in labour migration and trading activities for centuries by bringing and taking farm and manu-factured products to and from neighbouring areas. Thus it is necessary to move away from the sedentary bias of previous writers to understand migration as important in Badagas' lives throughout history. Also, rather than isolating migration events in the Nilgiris as something out of the ordinary, an alternative perspective in this monograph is emphasis on their normality and interconnections.

Another migration topic is the relocation of Sri Lankan Tamil refugees, also known as Ceylon Tamils or Jaffna Tamils. They are Tamil people of Sri Lankan origin whose ancestors were recruited in the 19th century from the Madras Presidency to work on plantations in British Ceylon. Ethnic conflict in Sri Lanka since the 1980s has resulted in their migration to India, although repatriation of refugees from India to Sri Lanka has also taken place (Dasgupta 2003). A large proportion of Sri Lankan Tamil refugees resettled in the Nilgiris, and has since become one of the largest groups of migrants, estimated by Heidemann (1997) to have numbered over 100,000 in the 1980s. The Tamil Nadu Government placed the refugees there on the assumption they would find employment in the tea industry, as they previously lived on plantations in Sri Lanka (Hockings 1999). Another reason is an ethnic and linguistic connection between Sri Lankan Tamils and Indian Tamils (Valatheeswaran and Rajan 2011). Despite the general trend of essentializing ethnic identity in the Nilgiris, Heidemann (1997) describes the Sri Lankan Tamil refugees in Tamil Nadu as a heterogeneous and complex group with regards to caste and place of origin. It is claimed 'these generally unskilled people have made themselves deeply unpopular with local inhabitants by their encroachment on Badaga and other farmland, squatting in Badaga villages, aggressive politicizing, and evident liaisons with and protection by Tamil government officials in the district' (Heidemann 1997; Hockings 1999, p. 266). Hockings (1999) questions whether Badagas can maintain a strong ethnic identity in light of the economic and political pressures of the increasing populations of migrants, as they have not been the numerically dominant group in the Nilgiris during the 20th century.

The repatriation also created complicated issues for the refugees concerning iden-tity and quality of life. These include coming to terms with displacement from Sri Lanka and its consequences; citizenship, as the children of the refugees born in India are registered as citizens of Sri Lanka (the Indian Government refuses to give them refugee status, permanent resident status or citizenship because it expects them to repatriate; and, in some cases, births, marriages, and deaths have not been offi-cially recorded in refugee camps); and life in refugee camps (Dasgupta 2003). The younger generation born in India might identify as Sri Lankan Tamils but consider themselves culturally and linguistically Indian as they regard life, culture and habits in India as routine and normal, and are part of local society (George et al. 2015, 2016; Valatheeswaran and Rajan 2011). Some refugees have expressed a desire to remain in India whereas others to return to Sri Lanka. Many factors contribute to ambivalent attitudes including the complexity of the repatriation process, family connections in Sri Lanka, duration of stay in India, educational and livelihood opportunities, perceived safety in Sri Lanka, and economic, political, and social support from Sri Lanka (George et al. 2015, 2016; Valatheeswaran and Rajan 2011). Younger people born in India are more likely to express a preference to remain, as they feel socially connected even though they regard Sri Lanka as their motherland (George et al. 2015, 2016; Valatheeswaran and Rajan 2011). These studies highlight the need to explore the complex notions of identity among migrants in India.

The online conversations by Badagas analysed in Chapter "Badagas Going Digital" show they are currently undergoing their 'second wave of migration' (as they put it) as they relocate to nearby towns and cities to escape declining incomes and living standards in the Nilgiris. As there is likely no single reason which can explain the motives behind their rural-to-urban migration, other changes not mentioned in the Internet forum might also be important, for example a labour surplus caused by agricultural intensification, livelihood diversification, and rising population density in India. Badagas writing in the forum were concerned about the consequences of the migration such as abandonment and neglect of customs and traditions; demographic change in villages; non-Badagas settling in the Badaga community with different ways of living; and the sale of houses, land, and tea estates which violates family inheritance customs. They worried that the established way of life was being challenged, and could lead to the demise of Badagas, a pessimistic outlook for the future. They were largely against rural-to-urban migration with one-sided and protectionist arguments. While the existence of problems for rural and urban areas as a result of migration cannot be denied, it should not be viewed as a problem per se. It is important to accept that it is probably inevitable, has benefits as well as drawbacks, and that migration and being Badaga are too complex for such monolithic classification. Therefore, further research is necessary to accommodate some of the complexities glossed over in the forum debates and academic literature.

The study reported here attempts, with sensitivity, to fill the gap in the literature by giving voice to myriad migration experiences. It unpacks the complexity of migrants' lives in Bangalore as they attempted to uphold some sense of autonomy and heritage as Badaga while also becoming functional members of an urban society in search of a better future. Specifically, the study sought answers to the following questions: What was the background and situation of the migrants? How did they self-identify and understand themselves as Badagas? How was their life and quality of life in the city? What happens when people leave the Nilgiri Hills, the social context in which they grow up and identify as Badaga, and move to a new environment where the former tenets of their identities and life quality no longer exist? What opportunities and challenges do they face? Answering these questions through examining the lived experiences of migration should paint a comprehensive picture of what it means to be Badaga in urban areas. The findings also have broader implications. Rural-to-urban migrants deal with everyday life associated with India's development and urbanisation over relatively short time periods, which enables scrutiny on a personal level, as similar changes might occur gradually in the Nilgiris in the coming years. As migration has implications for quality of life in origin and destination locations, the study helps to identify any issues and assistance needed, and how positive impacts of migration and urbanization can be maximised while negative impacts minimised. For those involved in planning for the future of the Nilgiris and cities, understanding rural-to-urban migrants is crucial for successful social policy. The study, then, is also an attempt to understand the complex relationship between migration and quality of life, an important endeavour considering that India holds a large number of urban dwellers and will continue to do so.

The research focuses on migrants born in the Nilgiri Hills, although several interviews were also conducted with second-generation migrants to refine and saturate a theme in the analysis (Becoming City Badaga, p.87). The methodology of the study and its theoretical underpinning (symbolic interactionism) are detailed in Chapter "Methodology". The interviews with Badagas in Bangalore spanned a wide array of themes which have been categorised as: (a) Departing the Nilgiri Hills, (b) The Promised Land: Living in Bangalore, (c) Being Badaga, and (d) Becoming City Badaga. Collectively, these themes and their descriptions comprise the migrants' shared experiences and interpretations as Badagas living in the city, particularly in connection with identities and quality of life. Below is an account of each theme which represents a broad consensus among the participants unless described otherwise, with examples of quotes from the interviews.

Departing the Nilgiri Hills

All of the migrants had grown up in the Nilgiri Hills, and moved to Bangalore as adults. Some had also lived in other cities, for example Chennai, Hyderabad, and Mumbai. Length of residence in Bangalore varied in the sample, one-year to more than thirty.

We discussed the reasons why they had left their villages in the Nilgiris. Agriculture as a profession did not sustain a decent standard of living. It was not an option for them because of low incomes, unpredictable costs, and risks. Tea cultivation and the running of tea estates were described in the interviews as 'a struggle', 'doomed', 'unguaranteed income', and 'not worth it'. One interviewee described his family's circumstances:

> My family's tea plot in Ooty is not running well. Ten years ago, we earned 25 Rupees per kg; now it's only 2! How can we survive on that? Barely enough money to make ends meet. It's dreadful for me to continue in those footsteps. I love Ooty, but I can't stay...there is no job, no money. I keep telling my parents they should leave too. (Male, 36)

The above extract describes the financial difficulties in the interviewee's family, the prime reason for his migration to the city. Similar to the other migrants, he interpreted his relocation to Bangalore as inevitable, and although we talked about the motives of migration, he conceded that ultimately there was no alternative but to leave.

The interviewees complained about limited employment opportunities in the Nilgiris which they attributed to its economic backwardness and sluggish agricultural sector. Villages and towns were not devoid of business activities, but they tended to be small-scale family enterprises employing family members and non-locals willing to work for low wages, and few were owned by Badagas. They also complained about limited government and private sector initiatives supporting business development, economic growth, and job generation, as they thought the Badaga community and local areas had been side-lined in the country's development plans. However, they also blamed Badagas for missed opportunities over the years. A contrast was made with Tibetans who arrived in Ooty in the 1970s. As traders of Tibetan handicrafts they established the Tibetan Market (near the Botanical Gardens), which is profitable and reputed. They complimented their ability to establish a thriving community and business from scratch by taking on the challenges they faced. Said the oldest Badaga in the sample (age 61):

> We [Badagas] are poor compared to what we were and what we could have become. The outsiders came and settled and have more money than us. We have not grown in the same way. They are doing well in Ooty, but look at us—we scratch our heads, and slave away on farcical farming. They bought up all the land right under our noses! If we had shown more initiative, things would be much different. (Male, 61)

The quote above referred to non-Badagas generally. He attributed the dire situation of Badagas to their reliance on agriculture and disregard of entrepreneurship. He praised other people in the Nilgiris for getting on in life, establishing businesses, and acquiring resources for living, and portrayed Badagas as naïve and unable to adapt to modernity.

The interviewees described their migration as social mobility, a desire to improve their situation by moving forward in life to new and exciting possibilities. Many jobs in the Nilgiris were menial and unskilled. The city offered a wide array of professional careers and employment, especially for graduates—a key reason for their migration. The majority of them sought career and personal development prospects in the city's booming business and financial sectors, and several were employed in leading Indian and international companies. They had not encountered major difficulties finding work in Bangalore, and enjoyed higher incomes. A migrant summarised his career progression in Bangalore:

> I got a job as a Customer Service Rep in a call centre. Six months later, I was in a training workshop to be a supervisor. After probation, I got promoted to be my team's manager. Now, I am a middle manager. I am not stopping here! (Male, 26)

The above quote describes his career progression in Bangalore, and ambitions for the future. Such opportunities—promotion from an entry-level to middle-management position, and access to a management training programme—were said to be almost non-existent in the Nilgiris.

The interviewees willingly disclosed their monthly earnings which ranged 20,000 Rupees (recent college graduate) to 100,000 (senior manager); in comparison, farmers in the Nilgiris typically earned less than 5000 at the time of the initial interviews in 2010, relatively poor in economic terms. Farmers made hardly enough profit to live, and some lost money as their tea plantations were financially unviable. Their quality of life was a cause of concern for everyone. An interviewee described his feelings about problems in his village:

> It makes me sad when I think about the greatness we fell from and the hole we are now languishing in. Things are getting worse by the day; it is depressing. (Male, 49)

The situation at the time of the interviews was compared to the past. The 1980s and 1990s were labelled by the interviewees as 'The Good Old Days' when agriculture was profitable, and Badagas enjoyed a comparatively high standard of living in terms of income level, availability of employment, and ease by which they were able to satisfy their needs and wants. Said another migrant:

> My father graduated from a top university when few of us went to university. He declined a job offer from the city government to return to his father's tea estate. Believe it or not, profits then were much higher than working in Bangalore! Back in his time he made so much money—as much as 10,000 [Rupees] a week—he didn't know what to do with it all! (Male, 22)

The above comment describes the past, when tea cultivation was profitable. It also reveals longitudinal change in rural-to-urban migration: While he had migrated to Bangalore for economic prosperity, his father had returned to the Nilgiris from the city for the same reason several decades previously. It also shows rural-to-urban migration is not a recent phenomenon among Badagas.

The interviewees could not explain the details and causes of the agricultural issues. They said incomes had been hampered by low market prices of tea, high production costs, and inefficient small- and medium-size farms, but were unable to elaborate these explanations. They blamed farmers, including their own families, for failure to critically examine and improve agricultural procedures, lack of planning for the future, and unresponsiveness to changing economic and societal circumstances. The following reflection by an interviewee sums up this viewpoint:

> A long time ago we used to boast we were the greatest. We were certainly the wealthiest. And, my generation was the first to become teachers, doctors, and alike. But those good times were filled with naivety, an idea they were forever. We never imagined it would have become this bad. Frankly, it's shocking…embarrassing even. (Male, 55)

However, not everyone wanted to leave the Nilgiris. Some people preferred to stay and continue the status quo, as agriculture had always been their livelihood and way of life, and it was difficult to find alternatives; another reason was respect for ancestral land and tradition. We also discussed positive aspects of life in the Nilgiris. They reasoned Badagas were relatively well-off compared to many other rural people, especially in states such as Bihar, Madhya Pradesh, Orissa, and Uttar Pradesh. They said some small-holders in other tea-growing areas in India survived only with hand-outs from the Government, and the poverty and child labour in the northern states of Assam and Bengal did not exist in the Nilgiris. Though many Badagas struggled to make ends meet, the vast majority were able to satisfy at least their basic needs with sufficient resources for living—food, water, basic necessities, education, healthcare, and housing. Families were able to grow their own vegetables for consumption; and, at the time of the interviews, rice was available throughout Tamil Nadu at low prices because of government subsidies (about one Rupee per kilogram), and electricity and water charges were low. Also, Badagas, unlike many Indians, tend to be home- and land-owners as they have inherited land and property, although not everyone. A wide range of inexpensive goods were available in nearby shops, markets, and towns, but expensive goods were out of reach for many people, and prices had risen in recent years. Quality of life in the Nilgiris was also captioned as beautiful natural scenery: abundant nature, fresh air, magnificent landscapes, and multiple sides of weather. Therefore, while the interviewees complained of challenging living conditions, they also reasoned Badagas fared better than many other Indians. As one participant put it:

> Well, here's my list: We have roofs over our heads, food on our tables, and clothes on our backs. We have colour TVs with a 100 channels! No Badaga begs or sleeps on the streets! (Male, 31)

They also valued the strong sense of community in the Nilgiri Hills, a feeling that everyone mattered, and that by being a member of the Badaga community, they were contributing to something worthwhile. Everyone in surrounding homes and areas considered themselves to be a big family which they cared about and felt engaged and connected with. Being part of a close and caring community was conducive to enjoying life, and enabled them to cope when things became difficult. They missed these social relationships in the city, yet they also valued the freedom, independence, and individualism of being there.

Some of the men had moved to Bangalore for further and higher education opportunities, and stayed in the city after graduation. In their view, the availability and quality of its colleges were superior to the Nilgiris. Bangalore is reputed throughout India for its educational institutions; some have global acclaim. Coimbatore, a city 228 km from the Nilgiris, has more than 150 colleges and universities, and is another popular choice for students. Even so, the majority of Badagas study in local or nearby colleges for the following reasons: Low tuition and living expenses, public perceptions that local colleges were satisfactory, concerns about the urban environment, and even ignorance and disregard for education by some families. The interviewees that had studied in Bangalore said they had supportive parents including some who had borrowed money to fund their studies.

The Promised Land: Living in Bangalore

The interviewees painted a picture of contentment with life in Bangalore. Positive talk of the city emphasised employment and career opportunities, convenient-living, and leisure activities. The migrants were financially-independent, and material goods had become important to them. Disposable incomes and spending power, along with availability and diversity of consumer products, had led to their adoption of a consumer culture: new types and sites of consumption and everyday displays of goods and wealth, a materialist orientation disconnected from their previous hold on frugality. Consumption in the city had also led to novels forms of leisure, as Bangalore's department stores, shops, and shopping malls were attractive not only because of the goods on sale but also the clean, spacious, and air-conditioned sites for social experiences. Said one participant:

> Bangalore leads the way in glamour and glitz! Forum Mall on Hosur Road has become vital in my life. I go with friends several times a week; we grab a coffee or McDonalds, stroll round, chat. It's good 'brain medicine' to deal with the stress of my job. There are no malls in Ooty. (Male, 25)

His consumption sites had shifted from small stores in the Nilgiri Hills to shopping malls, coffee shops, and fast food restaurants, a prominent feature of his social life in the city. However, these sites meant more to him than consumption and materialism; they were new social spaces and forms of leisure. He also regarded the shopping mall to be important for his emotional health, thereby connecting consumption to wellbeing.

They said a hallmark of being Badaga was a simple way of life and disinterest in materialism. Badagas in the Nilgiri Hills were described as a content and happy community because they embraced simple lifestyles, and were satisfied with what they had. Conditions in rural villages, although a world away from the city, were said to be sufficient to uphold satisfaction with life. They said happiness is not something one has but something who one is, a perspective of looking spiritually inward and outward through contemplation and inner reflection rather than in material goods which were regarded as illusionary and relatively unimportant. This perspective was entwined with Hindu beliefs, especially Karma. However, a contradiction was apparent in the explanation. They had adopted a consumer culture in Bangalore yet upheld themselves as detractors of materialism. When asked for clarification, they interpreted their consumption as different to others in Bangalore, a distinctive 'Badaga consumerism' underscored by strong views about the ownership of goods as necessities of living rather than symbols of wealth, social position, and status. The interviewees disapproved of 'conspicuous consumption', and did not regard themselves as being at the forefront of fashions, brand names or status symbols. Indeed, all of the Badagas I met in Bangalore were dressed casually and plainly, and they appeared typical or average in their appearance with jeans, pullovers, sneakers, and sandals devoid of brand names and high-end consumer goods, although they all adopted Western styles, explained by the interviewees as a marriage of city and Badaga values. Even so, they did not accept the downplaying of materialism without qualm, as it was pointed out their migration had been an attempt to better themselves in a material sense.

There was, however, a downside to life in Bangalore. Cost of living constrained their choices and lives in the city, especially expensive property rents. Only three of the interviewees owned an apartment or house; the others rented accommodation, typically a single-bedroom in a shared house at a cost of Rs. 5000–10000 monthly. As exemplified in the complaint below, while their incomes were sufficient to financially support daily-living, as everyday necessities were affordable, many things were too expensive. Even so, all of the interviewees acknowledged their standard of living in the city was higher than in the Nilgiris, and about half of the sample was able to save money to remit to their families, typically several thousand Rupees monthly. And, although they complained of affordability, they did not consider themselves in poverty, and none lived in squatter settlements, shantytowns or slums even though these types of housing existed in Bangalore.

> Things can be cheap, things can be costly. The price tag on imported items will blow your mind. Prices have gone up a lot. My salary is not low but I have to think twice when buying…I don't spend much when I am with my friends, I just window shop. It's possible to live here cheaply, though…I have just enough to get by. (Male, 19)

Shops and services (e.g. auto-drivers, bus conductors, landlords, street vendors) sometimes charged them higher prices than Bangaloreans, prejudice directed at migrants based on stereotypes that they were professional workers earning comparatively high salaries. However, discrimination and inequality were not perceived to be major problems in Bangalore, as they rarely encountered unequal treatment and were socially-accepted by others. They held favourable, positive attitudes towards Bangaloreans, and praised their acceptance of difference. One interviewee even claimed Bangalore's position as a cultural melting pot was an exemplar for other countries to learn how to achieve social harmony within multicultural communities. However, they had received complaints from elderly locals about the city's dramatic change from its former status as a peaceful and quiet locale, criticism targeted at migrants generally and not them specifically. Another interviewee said Badaga migrants in other places, for example Kavundampalayam in Coimbatore, had created tensions with local residents, but I decided not to investigate the point further as it was beyond the scope of the study.

Working in the city was challenging with long commutes and working-hours, high performance expectations such as meeting targets and deadlines, and relationship issues with colleagues. The migrants talked about work-related pressure, burnout, insomnia, and the impossibility of a work-life balance. About one-third of them said their job was exhausting as they spent all of their time either working or resting from work and had limited time and energy for other activities. At the time of the initial interviewees in 2010, Bangalore's economy had been affected by a global financial crisis triggered by valuation and liquidity problems in the U.S. banking system and housing market in 2008. A recession hit Bangalore in 2009 with financial and job losses, especially in the information technology industry following a decline in demand for exports and services. Two of the interviewees had lost their jobs, and several others had reduced salaries, working hours, and perks. The migrants feared job security, and several had cancelled or postponed financial plans such as a mortgage application and setting up a business. One man described his unemployment during that time:

> I was an engineer for G.E. It was a good job, but we were laid off at short notice in early 2009. I couldn't find another job for three-months. I tried my best, but few were recruiting. I was in a difficult position. I didn't return to the Nilgiris…I was too ashamed to tell my parents. Thank god my savings covered my rent. Now I work for Rolls Royce; it's okay, but not as good as before. (Male, 28)

Another commonality among the men was an intention to reside in the Nilgiri Hills in the future. Their migration to Bangalore was not considered to be permanent; living in the city was regarded as a home away from home, transient and secondary. Some of the men were optimistic about being able to return in the near future; others envisioned a lengthier wait. The desire to live there was based on several reasons: A sense of belongingness to the place they regarded as their motherland; to be with family, friends, and Badagas; and to enjoy its natural environment and scenic beauty, conducive to a fulfilling and satisfying life. But they were unable to support themselves in the Nilgiris because of limited income and employment. However, three of the men, residents in Bangalore for more than a decade, made their preference to stay in the city very clear. They felt settled in Bangalore, and thought the Badaga community in the Nilgiri Hills had changed markedly since they had left. They said they might not be able to readjust. They were also concerned about the limited availability of goods and services as their lifestyles and needs had shifted. Even so, they visited regularly, had not sold their inherited land and property, and still paid village tax (an honorary, informal tax). These continuing ties were important in their lives; they did not reject the salience of the Nilgiri Hills in their lives but they also felt a strong sense of belonging in Bangalore. One of them said:

> I think of myself as a Bangalorean now, granting a large part of me will always remain there [the Nilgiris]. Jeez...I've been here for donkey's years, a family and house here now, my birth place is less on my mind. But I am still a Badaga, and I keep up-to-date with my village's comings and goings. (Male, 57)

Other challenges in Bangalore were regarded as typical frustrations of daily life: Inadequate services, poor roads, electricity outages, water-shortages, construction work, pollution, traffic jams, and lack of greenery. Economic and population growth had put considerable pressure on urban infrastructure and resources which had not kept up with the city's development. These issues impinged on quality of life, as shown in the complaint below, but were regarded as minor inconveniences:

> The power blacks out a few times a day. We've been without power for an hour today. It's a short time, but we can't do many things. I sometimes work from home, and can't do my work; my wife cannot prepare dinner. We can't even go out because the shops are left high and dry. (Male, 42)

Being Badaga

Being Badaga was the essence of who they were, the fundamental basis of being human. It was central to their sense of self: How they understood themselves and others, their interaction with the social world, and ultimately how they made their way through life. It was also expressed in relation to others, "us-ness" with other Badagas. In this way, being Badaga was described as both an inner feeling, the foundation of thinking and state of mind, and an outward feeling of engaging with the world at large, which imbued their lives with meaning and enjoyment, as illustrated in the quotes below:

> I love being a Badaga, it's really who I am...my mind, my thoughts, my essence, my life. But I want to state categorically that I am also proud [to be a Badaga] because I was born there, it's my motherland, a special place where we are the same and love each other. (Male, 31)

This is a real issue. I am a Badaga, and will always be a Badaga by heart. It's my true character, deep in the depths of my soul. It comes from God, my ancestors, my people. Us Badagas are a big family…and we are all on the same page, so-to-speak. (Male, 37)

Distinct lines ran between 'Badaga' and 'non-Badaga'. Being a native of the Nilgiri Hills, and 'belonging' to its Badaga community, were important. Thus, being Badaga was ascribed at birth, in virtue of being born in the Nilgiris, as the interviewees expressed a strong emotional accord with their villages and community, regarded as their 'motherland'. Though they were living in the city, their identification with the Badaga community in the Nilgiri Hills remained strong and central.

Another anchor was family: parents, siblings, villagers, and ancestors—Badagas past and present. The interviewees explained they were family- and community-orientated, as their feelings, thinking, and behaviour were embedded in the social, valued as a key ingredient of a fulfilling and satisfying life. They regretted separation from family and friends while in Bangalore. The men visited their ancestral home monthly or bi-monthly, and trips were planned to coincide with family events and days of festivity; and their relatives occasionally visited them in Bangalore for several days to weeks at a time. For many interviewees, the round trip home was completed in a weekend (departing on Friday evening after work, and returning on Monday morning before work) which was exhausting because of the overnight bus journeys on Friday and Sunday which meant they went directly to work after arriving on Monday morning from Bangalore's Kempagowda Bus Station, Majestic. The trip was significant, the 'highlight of the month', as they valued the collective: Family, village, and community. They talked about 'collective happiness', a shared and combined sense of the wellbeing of Badagas as a group, from individual to family, community, and beyond. 'Collective happiness' was defined as the general mood of the community, a collaboration among family and friends in which everyone worked together for the common good. Individual happiness also stemmed from social footing, as to be happy involved the happiness of others. Similarly, any problem which impinged on an individual was interpreted as a problem of the family and community.

The interviewees made reference to their ancestry, and I asked about their knowledge of the history of Badagas. They had limited knowledge of the topic beyond the history of their immediate families, but were familiar with some aspects of Badaga folklore. They all believed the migration story of their ancestors originating from the former Mysore region several centuries previously. However, they were unable to describe or explain it, and seemed to know almost nothing about it. Even so, the migration was taken for granted as factual. I also probed their awareness of writings about Badagas. Most of them were aware of the existence of books about Badagas, but only two could name one of the books or authors, and only one had read one. An interesting comment came from the daughter of an interviewee when she was asked by her father, a participant in the study, to fetch *Kindreds of the Earth* from their bookshelf. As a second-generation migrant (she had lived in Bangalore since early childhood), her knowledge of Badagas was very limited. She appreciated the book as an opportunity to find out more, and enjoyed discovering about her heritage. Based on our discussions, I decided to conduct several interviews with Badagas that had grown up outside the Nilgiris as second-generation migrants, described at the end of the chapter.

Also important to being Badaga were morals, principles, and personal values which represented rules of thumb for how they lived their lives. Badagas were singled out by the interviewees for their unique philosophy of life. 'Doing the right thing' was said to be their guiding principle, defined by them as 'doing one's duty of being good', 'honesty and truthfulness', 'meeting social responsibilities', 'friendliness and hospitality', 'going above and beyond the call of duty', and 'accountability to oneself'. The philosophy imbued direction for the choices they made about how to live through assessing the moral quality of their actions. However, it was seen as a struggle between good and bad, as 'doing the right thing' was not always easy to do or judge, especially in Bangalore where they faced an inordinate number of difficult decisions. But while a principled life in accordance with these personal convictions did not guarantee perfect integrity, it guided them to do their best and avoid feelings of guilt and shame. Regarded as a kind of Badaga 'philosophy of life', these principles also etched out a roadmap for living the good life, as satisfaction with life was linked with doing good, and living the 'right way' was synonymous with being content and at peace with oneself. The interdependence of morals and wellbeing in this way was set against a background of their relationship with God, Hinduism, and Karma, as they believed a life of contentment fitted into place for those who genuinely respected and did good deeds for others. Thus, happiness and wellbeing were seen as outcomes of the totality of their actions in the past, present, and future, some of which were shaped long before they were born through cycles of birth and death.

Fluency in Badagu was another building block of being Badaga. Conversing in the language differentiated them and non-Badagas, and was regarded as synonymous with coming from the community in the Nilgiri Hills. Although literacy in English and Tamil was important, Badagu was the principal means of communication in homes and villages and deemed necessary for full participation in their culture and society. It enabled them to truly express inner feelings and thoughts, and nurtured common understanding, a sense of grounding as Badaga. For these reasons, Badagu was an authentic and central pillar of being Badaga. However, the migrants were living in Bangalore and used English in daily life and the workplace. I asked them to weigh up the utility of Badagu, Tamil, and English in their lives. Badagu was primarily for communication with family and Badagas, and participation in community events, ceremonies, and festivals, whereas English and Tamil were essential for living outside the Nilgiris and communication with non-Badagas; all languages were seen as necessary and complementary. Fluency in English was deemed important for cultural competence in Bangalore and beyond, and for this reason they believed all Badagas should acquire a good command of English; poor language skills limited career and life opportunities. Badagu was not taught outside the home environment (unlike Tamil which was taught in schools administered by the Government of Tamil Nadu). Badagu was very important to them, and they cherished opportunities in the city to converse in it, but their lives in Bangalore had shown them a good command of English was essential.

The interviewees elaborated on being Badaga in Bangalore. Relocating to the city was conveyed as a vehicle of personal growth. They still maintained a resolute foothold with the Nilgiri Hills, but had also developed a deep sense of attachment to the city, a new place which had gradually become more personal. They articulated being Badaga as flexible and changing, as concurrent connections with both rural and urban had given rise to hybridity—a minority subgroup with similarities and distinctions to Badagas in the Nilgiri Hills and non-Badagas in Bangalore. This new type of Badaga, which some of them labelled 'City Badaga', was characterised as a collective of like-minded people with similarities in their backgrounds and changing circumstances based on assimilation of urban culture and lifestyle. Further discussions about the meanings of being a City Badaga revealed they considered themselves subtly different to Badagas at large by having a bicultural understanding of the customs, social norms, and world views of both rural and urban, a dual grounding on the Nilgiris and Bangalore. They felt able to navigate and maintain their lives and relationships in both cultural worlds without having to choose between them. Thus, being City Badaga was viewed positively as an enriched view of life and the world. In Bangalore, they put on their 'City Badaga' hat and embraced the urban way of life; however, in the Nilgiris, it was juxtaposed with 'Nilgiri Badaga', a way of doing aligned more with its norms regarding attitudes, behaviours, and choices. They justified the identity flexibility as a strategy of self-presentation to others through regulating the image they thought they needed to portray in each locality to address relevant expectations and needs respectively, pointing to their fluid interpretations of being Badaga. Below is an example of identity flexibility by a migrant working as a financial advisor in the city.

> I'm a City Badaga here all of my waking time, seven days a week, morning to night. My job is a financial advisor. I wear this suit, this name tag, and act like I am one! Most people just see me as another city guy; my clients just see me as 'the financial advisor'. But when I return to the Nilgiris, I put on my Badaga clothes, speak Badagu, and say the things…behave the way…they expect. I return to my old ways, completely different to here. (Male, 28)

City Badaga was objectified in terms of material distinctions, geographical separation from the Nilgiri Hills, differential access to income and consumption, and greater emphasis on urban culture and Westernised lifestyles. Individualism and individual autonomy—greater personal freedom to pursue one's own interests, goals, and personal choice of lifestyle—were also central to City Badaga as they tended to put themselves first and make their own decisions in Bangalore, in contrast to their former selves in the Nilgiris which were more cooperative and interdependent.

The interviewees found it easier in our interviews to articulate the meanings of Nilgiri Badaga than City Badaga, which suggests the former was more clearly delineated in their minds and the latter was abstract and ambiguous. Although both were separated as either-or terms (either 'City Badaga' or 'Nilgiri Badaga'), their differences were subtle, overlapping and blurred rather than absolute. Cultural continuities between Bangalore and the Nilgiris were emphasised, as they thought both identities were unified by similarities more than divided by differences. These similarities enabled a comfortable adaption to city life, and also legitimised 'City Badaga', as reflected in the following comments:

> There is no written rule which tells us what we should do or believe in. Yes, we [City Badaga] have our quirks, our points of view, but I don't think we do things that unusually. You know, most of us Indians are Hindus, not much difference, just a little. Actually, it helped me to settle in. (Male, 31)

> Any gap or likeness is only in our heads. Anyone can be different depending on what you look at. Only after leaving Kotagiri did I begin to question who I am. You see, a Badaga in my village is nothing special, everyone is the same. But in Bangalore I feel I am different, but also the same. I also feel like it now whenever I visit my home [in the Nilgiris]. I am seeing myself in new ways. (Male, 30)

But the differences, although subtle, were important. Being City Badaga meant the shedding of some long-standing practices. In Bangalore they continued morning prayers, speaking Badagu (regular telephone conversations with parents), and listening to songs and music. Also, they returned to the Nilgiris as much as possible to participate in family and community events. However, most customs were not easily conducted outside the family home; they were described as interlocked with village, society, and the totality of the Nilgiri Hills. For example, homes have shrines or clearly demarcated places of worship, and religious events involve the participation of the entire family and community. Also, limited leisure time hindered the practice of time-consuming practices such as preparation of traditional meals, unsuitable for their fast-paced city lifestyles. Discontinuing this precedent while in Bangalore was described as a sense of loss, accompanied by feelings of anxiety, guilt, and shame. They regretted not being able to participate more often in ceremonies, which they interpreted as failure to live in accordance with Hinduism. However, while they acknowledged the urge to uphold conventions which they considered essential to being Badaga, they also made an effort to embrace the protocol necessary for successful living in the city. They also realised some aspects of Badaga culture were archaic and unnecessary in the city, as shown in the quote below. Thus, living in Bangalore had enabled them to experiment with new experiences, challenge prior conceptions, and sift through the past to uncover new ways of understanding the present.

> I love living as a Badaga, but I also have to match Bangalore. Let me give you an example. Let's say you got a job here, in this coffee shop. As an employee, your opinions should match those of your company. Your work duties should be in line too, say to meet your targets. If not, you will be fired. It's either kill or be killed. Yes, you can have your own ways, but they have to do what you have to do. It's the same as my life here. You need to give-and-take to get on in life. (Male, 50)

Some of the interviewees desired to facilitate change among Badagas, to 'bring them into the 21st century' as one put it. The migrants, culturally grounded in their place of origin, and yet armed with experience of the city, recognised their strengths and potential to improve the standing of the Badaga community in the Nilgiri Hills. They wanted to serve as mediators to forge links between the community and outside, and apply their experience and skills to tackle issues. Thus, migration was not just to have a better life for themselves but also to help Badagas at large, and identification as City Badaga had motivated them to use their new skills and position to improve the quality of life of Nilgiri Badagas, a kind of cross-border economics. Yet their desires to better the rural Badaga community seemed to be a future vision than a reality, as only two interviewees had taken action, namely helping to organise school trips for children to visit Bangalore, and sponsoring students' college fees.

Becoming City Badaga

I asked questions about their experiences of becoming City Badaga, acquisition of a new group identification. Identity change or flexibility was articulated as an ongoing process of personal growth, new ways of thinking and living and making sense of self and the world. Becoming City Badaga was just as much about exploring awareness of one's self as it was about acquainting with the propositions of urban life. It did not take place as a coercive effort but through subtle shifting perspectives of life, beginning before they had arrived in Bangalore by bringing into awareness that which was on the horizon, followed by the migration and then exploration of the new environment. Through participating in the city, testing for comfort and safety, dealing with the surprises they encountered, and honing attitudes and life skills during the initial months in Bangalore, they took hold of their new way of being—a realisation that they had to live and think in different ways to survive and succeed—and moved from feeling out of place in the city to feeling comfortable. Gradually, the self, as they saw it, became enriched with a new awareness of changing personal relations with society, a better understanding of how, and why, they were Badaga. The change was not a replacement of old with new but a reframing of previous experiences with novel ideas, a new philosophy of life. As the city gained a more prominent hold, they were able to dig deeply into their inner selves by questioning how they understood and went about life. As they accepted who they were becoming, from an position they once had as Nilgiri Badaga to a new presence as city folk, they came to acknowledge and accept themselves as 'City Badaga'. Thus, becoming City Badaga was described as a journey through different perspectives of self-understanding and the world; and out of this came the emergence of a new sense of self fully invested in both past and present. As fully-fledged City Badaga, they felt established on their new circumstances, and proud of gaining something valuable, not only new skills and confidence but an entirely new way of being. Therefore, the boundary in-between Nilgiri Badaga and City Badaga was an interface of reflection and negotiation with oneself in different social contexts, and a process of changing self-definition as Badaga, and not a site of division, as the interviewees acted out both identities:

Man, I used to be a sleepwalker…on autopilot. Not good, uh? I shifted to B'lore, I was asking myself why I do things this way or that way. The more I understood, the more I got on with guys here. We are all from different places. What makes me misty-eyed is how my different thoughts came together. The 'me' that has always been me is still here, but I have improved, I feel different, I feel like a new man. (Male, 25)

Come to think of it, it was tricky. It [the migration] triggered me to mull things over. I think the change-over in how I see myself is an up-sway on my life. It's difficult to express, but

> basically I now live in a conscious mode, I now have control over my life. I feel connected to my inner self—who I am, what I stand for. I have enjoyed the ride so-far. (Male, 30)

However, becoming City Badaga was difficult. Leaving the Nilgiri Hills was a sad time of parting and separation, the ending of a deep and personal relationship with a place crucial to their lives. Also, all of the interviewees encountered challenges adjusting to the city and letting go of the familiar and entrenched ways of being, at least initially. The realisation that becoming City Badaga was irreversible played on their conscience. Once the unfamiliar in Bangalore became familiar, they were in a position of not being able to go back to their former selves but also unsure of the outcome of going forward, as if one foot was on the gas pedal and another on the brakes. They toyed with the moral convictions of whether it was right and moral, even though they had no choice. However, these concerns turned out to be unfounded as only a few of the men had struggled to come to terms with the change, partly because they maintained a foothold with their residual culture by regularly visiting the Nilgiris and socializing with Badagas in Bangalore. Though they were initially apprehensive of identity flexibility, it later came across as a healthy reaction to their migration, as they came to see City Badaga not as a threat but as normative for city life, as if to say 'modern living is the thing to do'. Also, negative aspects of the migration were counterbalanced with its opportunities, as their time in Bangalore was cherished as a chance to better themselves and have an enriching and exciting life. Moreover, as the changing self was construed as a gradually increasing awareness and contact in the city, they distanced themselves from the notion of actively disowning Badaga culture or behaving wrongly for economic self-interest. They also pointed out the move to Bangalore was for good reasons, and that non-involvement in the new surroundings was not an option. Thus they posited an alternative notion of right and wrong which hinged on whether they were wearing the City Badaga or Nilgiri Badaga hat: In Bangalore, being City Badaga was the right way to be to fit in, whereas being Nilgiri Badaga was suitable for the Nilgiris. In other words, they reported positive and negative connotations of both identities depending on social context, rather than one being right or wrong.

The key to being content with oneself in Bangalore was openness to new experiences. It was important to accept and embrace different ways of being and living, even if they did not fully agree with them, and to work around difficulties, which meant making compromises and reaching a common ground between their new lives and the assumptions they challenged. Feelings of us-ness with other Badagas in the city were important for coping successfully with challenges, and helped to ease the transition from rural to urban. Each interviewee had a small circle of close friends in Bangalore and nearby cities who cared about them, and whose company they enjoyed. Being with other Badagas who understood their predicament afforded a sense of emotional comfort and reassurance. The social support also represented a safe space in which they could be City Badaga and experiment with self, essentially validating it as a legitimate existence. It also shows how their understandings of identities were intersubjective, perceived and interpreted in shared conscious interaction. Friendships in Bangalore with non-Badagas were regarded as more common, complex and diverse than in the Nilgiri Hills, and involved social acquaintances of other castes and regions, unlike in the Nilgiris where they were predominantly Badaga- and family-orientated.

Family support was important. Living in the city was fraught with emotional challenges which intensified when the men became aware of being in a transient state between Nilgiri Badaga and City Badaga; they knew they were continuing down a one-way path, a point of no return. Support and reassurance from family were interpreted as permission to do whatever was needed to make a life in the city. Whereas most of their family members held positive views of urban lifestyles and modern life, some were described as traditional-minded which the interviewees interpreted as forbiddenness to fully partake in urban life. A minority had encountered negativity from parents or family members concerning some aspect of their new lives in the city, especially the extent to which they imbibed individualism. They criticised the older generation for a contradiction in their wants, as they wanted to see their children succeed but also wanted things to remain the same. Conservatism by family and others put the interviewees at the centre of a tug-of-war as they found it difficult to satisfy the expectations of both family and the city; identity flexibility was a way to balance these opposites, although it did not solve every issue. The quote below, for example, reveals a mismatch between the expectations and interests of an interviewee and his parents.

> I love my family to pieces. But when I told them I wanted to study fashion design, they persuaded me to do something else. To please my father, I am doing a business diploma. But I really love fashion. Life there [in the Nilgiris] is simple and closed...my family is not in the 'real world'...they just don't understand...geez, my family has really screwed me up! (Male, 18)

The young man had his own hopes and dreams but he was also expected to submit to his family's expectations. He sacrificed his education and career goals to please his parents which he told me he regretted. Yet disobeying his parents would have also led to guilt and worry. So abandoning his career dreams of being a fashion designer was counterbalanced by personal satisfaction of respecting his parents and performing duty for its own sake, living life in accordance with one's dharma and not only individual interests. It also served to keep the family together in harmony. The quote also shows migration decisions were not exclusively taken by him but also his family.

The interviewees had to tread carefully. That they considered themselves different to Badagas in the Nilgiri Hills carried the risk of being over identified with the outside. Some elders were described as conservative, critical of modernity, and fierce defenders of the status quo, a kind of border control by symbolic guards monitoring the boundary between Nilgiri Badaga and City Badaga. Some of the interviewees even worried they might be excluded from Badagas at large, and relegated to the fringe of society through stigmatisation and marginalization. Identity flexibility buffered the threat by showcasing their continuing affiliation with their place of origin and its way of life. However, rather than an illusion of harmony, they came to accept irreconcilable differences which involved treading a fine line. But was there really a boundary, and was it being monitored and protected? They referenced only a possible outcome, as none of the men had experienced hostility or marginalisation. However, cases of moral condenment and social exclusion were recalled by the interviewees to support their concerns. A notable example was intercaste marriage, a major conflict between traditional and modern. A marriage between Badagas involves an elaborate set of religious customs including substantive consultation with family and elders which are severed in intercaste marriage. Badagas believe the pollution impurity of an intercaste marriage causes permanent misfortune for the bride and groom and their families for future generations. The interviewees knew of examples of intercaste marriages among family and friends, and described the emotional toll, quoted below. One interviewee's family lost respectability and social standing in his village, and were teased and ridiculed:

> My brother married a Tamil women he met at work in Chennai. Folks in our village did not agree to it…When my brother and his wife visit [the Nilgiris], they [villagers] give him them the 'cold shoulder'. My parents have a tough time dealing with the gossip; when neighbours visit, it's the first thing they talk about, again and again. Every so often he asks for my opinion. But what can I do? (Male, 36)

I used theoretical sampling to probe long-term living in the city. Specifically, I conducted interviews with two second-generation migrants who had grown up in Coimbatore and had lived in several cities since adulthood, notably Bangalore, Chennai, and Hyderabad. They had also lived overseas during short-term work placements, including in the U.K. Similar to the first-generation migrants, they regarded themselves as Badagas and members of the Badaga community in the Nilgiri Hills. However, being Badaga was not as central in their lives; it was something they reflected on from time-to-time. Other identities were more salient such as being Tamilian, an ethnic group which speaks Tamil and traces their ancestry to Tamil Nadu; when others enquired about their lives and where they were from, they were likely to reply they were Tamilian and from Coimbatore rather than mentioning Badagas and the Nilgiris. When I asked one of them to arbitrarily rank the order of importance of his identities, he put 'Badaga' at the bottom of the list because it only came to mind when he talked to his parents and family, met other Badagas, and visited the Nilgiri Hills. Moreover, they did not feel they were a different subgroup of Badagas, unlike the rural-to-urban migrants who self-identified as City Badaga.

However, they expressed a strong accord with the Nilgiri Hills, their relatives, ancestral village, and villagers whom they considered to be extended family. They visited once every three or four years, and yearly when they were younger. During these visits they were welcomed, and felt as if they were being treated as Badagas, and older villagers remembered their families. Although participation in village life during these visits was not easy for them, they still felt part the village and its people. They had not experienced hostility or negative reactions from anyone in the Nilgiri Hills, except complaints about their infrequent visits and non-participation in village events. They also reported changing their actions to satisfy the expectations of others; however, unlike the rural-to-urban migrants, the change was played down as 'acting', similar to portraying a character in a play, and not identity flexibility, as they did not perceive themselves as bicultural. Rather, they described feelings of being a foreigner or outsider in the Nilgiri Hills, even though it was also regarded as their home. They certainly did not express a strong desire to live there, as they could only bear visiting for several days, in contrast to the majority of the first-generation migrants who expressed a strong intention to return.

Badagu was their mother-tongue which they had learnt from birth, the principal language used at home when they were growing up and communicating with their parents. Badagu played an important role in their lives as the language they knew best and with which they could truly express inner feelings and thoughts, even though they rarely conversed in it as adults. One of the interviewees said he often had to translate his thoughts from Badagu to English or Tamil because his way of thinking in Badagu was different to thinking in other languages, even though he used English most of the time. Thus he reasoned that he probably thinks more like a Badaga than a Tamilian, although he could not explain the difference. I asked him to clarify whether thinking in Badagu contradicted his comment that being Badaga did not come into daily thinking. Again, he found it difficult to articulate the notion of thinking differently in two languages, but explained that his feelings of being Badaga only rose to the fore when he met or spoke to other Badagas. One of the interviewees had married a Badaga from Coimbatore, and another was planning to get married to a Badaga in the near future. The reasons for choosing a Badaga wife included respect for their parents, and concerns about criticism from Badagas regarding intercaste marriage. The unmarried interviewee had spent considerable time contemplating the possibilities of his marriage, especially finding a suitable partner, and at the time of the interview his parents and relatives were searching for potential suitors. As he was concerned about his future wife's adaption to city life, he preferred someone fluent in English and with several years' study or life experience outside the Nilgiris.

Both of them had fewer Badaga friends than the first-generation migrants, and all of their close friends were non-Badagas. Their close friends were Tamilian, although in the work place they interacted with Indians from all over the country. They emphasised distinctions between Tamilian and non-Tamilian based on a social divide in Tamil Nadu while growing up, underpinned by political factors which date to the anti-Hindi agitations of Tamil Nadu. For the same reasons, they did not learn other languages when growing up in Coimbatore, another reason for their preference to socialise with Tamilians. They each had a small circle of Tamilian friends (about 5 people) who lived together in a shared house and worked in different companies, and they spent a significant amount of time together, supporting each other in the new places. These friends tended to be contacts made in Coimbatore prior to moving to the city, and not colleagues. The characteristics of the social group were described as: Tamilian, close friends, like-mindedness, and similar experiences and interests. In contrast, their close friends and housemates were more diverse when they worked overseas, and included Indians from various locations, and not only Tamilians (Indians in the same company they had met after arriving in the country, on overseas placements). At first they preferred to befriend Tamilians, but there were none in their work and living places, and so the composition of friendship groups was less controllable, unlike their situation in India when they were more selective. The main in-group when they had worked overseas was essentially a work group with social ties extending beyond work, socialising and living with Indian colleagues. Living and working with non-Tamilians nurtured feelings of indifference and appreciation, and improved their attitudes towards people from north India; it also meant they tended to self-identify as Indian and not Tamilian to others overseas. Prior to going overseas they tended to avoid contact with Indians from other states (and foreigners), whereas upon returning to India they made an effort to befriend them.

Concluding Summary

This chapter has detailed my interviews with rural-to-urban migrants in Bangalore about their experiences of leaving their villages in the Nilgiri Hills, living in the city, being Badaga, and the journey of becoming City Badaga.

Being Badaga was synonymous with living a satisfying life. Important were social relationships with family and others, and they talked about 'collective happiness' as a shared and combined sense of the wellbeing of Badagas as a whole, the general mood of the community in the Nilgiri Hills. Doing good in life according to morals was also valued. While a negative depiction of life quality in the Nilgiri Hills was a salient theme, the migrants painted a picture of contentment with life in Bangalore, particularly with employment, income, convenient-living, and access to education, based on notions of social mobility and personal growth. There was no evidence of prejudice against the migrants (which is sometimes reported in migration studies), such as barriers to healthcare or other essential services, anti-migrant discrimination, stereotyping, social exclusion, substandard housing, xenophobia, or the abuse of migrants' human rights. There was no evidence of any interference with their social and economic integration or limits to their opportunities in the city. The migration contributed to livelihoods in the Nilgiris by alleviating unemployment and providing remittances which presumably improved quality of life. The migration was circular as they continued to maintain strong links with their hometowns, a strong inter-connectedness of place of origin and destination. New interpretations of self which came out of experimenting with their Badaganess in the city, and new ways of making sense of life, were viewed positively. Thus material gains were only a part of the migrants' benefits from the rural-to-urban migration. These findings challenge the anti-migrant message by pessimists, such as those reported in the forum posts analysed in Chapter "Badagas Going Digital", with positive outcomes of migration.

A thread tying the themes together was a deep personal sense of being Badaga, and on this common background rested diversity and flexibility, as the study shows the various ways Badaga identities and quality of life change under the impact of migration. A key finding was changing notions of what it meant to be a member of their caste as they engaged the city, as being Badaga was malleable to context and social and economic concerns, and therefore in a state of flux. It revealed a new identification or collective, City Badaga, characterized by shared experiences of Badagas living in the city. The study also uncovered the conditions and processes by which Badagas constructed distinctions to others, and the contextual determinants of identity construction. The migrants put together new meanings of self through negotiating and reworking their beliefs and social practices of being Badaga, leading to personal change and new formulations of identities, the vanguard of living in a cosmopolitan urban setting. The point here is that symbolic interaction among Badagas and others in the city represented unique relationships between self and society which nurtured new understandings of who they were, and new images of similarity and difference between themselves and others. Important was the existence of identity flexibility, a creative adaptation to deal with new challenges and unforeseen contingencies; as the migrant Badagas shifted from their home setting to the city, it allowed them to preserve some aspects of their heritage in exchange for new allegiances to the city. Yet while all of the migrants who went to the city underwent some kind of identity change, the all-encompassing Badaganess remained, and so self was both persistent and changeable, and connections between new and old aspects of their identities were complex and mutually constitutive.

In summary, it is clear that Badagas, if such a category really exists, do not conform to the model of a bounded primitive society in the Nilgiris. A reified identity and quality of life according to customary cultural prescriptions is also challenged. Such simplification ignores the complex and diverse lived realities of people with a Badaga heritage. The findings reveal complicated, flexible, and pluralistic notions of identities and living circumstances which are thoroughly in flux and negotiated and contested across multiple spaces, characterised by openness and variation. Moreover, symbolic interactionism's focus on people as agentic, autonomous, and integral in creating their social world, and their own interpretations of their circumstances, shows the need to move beyond previous deterministic and functionalist writings. The next chapter develops this revisionist narrative further by essentially redefining the classificatory structure of 'Badaga', and rebalancing inequalities in its representation through revealing identities that are dynamic, fluid, and lived at interrelated multiple sites, which transcends old Euro-American stereotypes and the positivist fantasy in the literature. It also considers the limitations as well as future directions of these findings. In doing so, it attempts to paint a holistic picture of what it means to be Badaga in India today which should remove its old fashioned portrayal once and for all.

References

Belli Gowder, M. (1923–1941). A historical research on the hill tribes of the Nilgiris. Unpublished manuscript, Ketti, Nilgiris District, India.

Belli Gowder, M. (1938–41). Origin of the Badagas. Unpublished manuscript, Ketti, Nilgiris District, India.

Benbow, J. (1930). The Badagas–beliefs and customs. Bangalore, India: United Theological College.

Dasgupta, A. (2003). Repatriation of Sri Lankan refugees: Unfinished tasks. *Economic and Political Weekly, 38*(24), 2365–2367.

Emeneau, M. B. (1944–1946). *Kota texts: Parts 1–4* (Vol. 2). Berkely, CA: University of California Press.

Ferreira, J. (1603, April 1). A letter from Father Jacome Ferreira to the Vice-Provincial of Calicut.

George, M., Kliewer, W., & Rajan, S. (2015). Rather than talking in Tamil, they should be talking to Tamils: Sri Lankan Tamil refugee readiness for repatriation. *Refugee Survey Quarterly, 34*(2), 1–22.

George, M., Vaillancourt, A., & Rajan, S. (2016). Sri Lankan Tamil refugees in India: Conceptual framework of repatriation success. *Refuge, 32*(3), 73–83.

Heidemann, F. (1997). Immigrant labourers and local networks in the Nilgiri. In P. Hockings (Ed.), *Blue mountains revisited: Cultural studies on the Nilgiri hills* (pp. 148–163). New Delhi, India: Oxford University Press.

Hockings, P. (1980). *Ancient Hindu refugees: Badaga social history, 1550–1975*. The Hague, The Netherlands: Mouton Publishers.

Hockings, P. (1999). *Kindreds of the earth: Badaga household structure and demography*. New Delhi, India: SAGE Publications.

Hockings, P. (2013). *So long a saga: Four centuries of Badaga social history*. New Delhi, India: Manohar.

Karl, W. (1945). *The religion of the Badagas* (Unpublished B. D. dissertation). Serampore College, India.

Mandelbaum, D. G. (1955). The world and the world view of the Kota. In M. Marriott (Ed.), *Village India: Studies in the little community* (pp. 223–254). Chicago, IL: University of Chicago Press.

Mandelbaum, D. G. (1989). The Nilgiris as a region. In P. Hockings (Ed.), *Blue mountains: The ethnography and biogeography of a South Indian region* (pp. 1–19). New Delhi, India: Oxford University Press.

Richards, F. J. (1932). Cultural geography of the Wynaad. *The Indian Antiquary: A Journal of Oriental Research, 61*(170–4), 195–7.

Valatheeswaran, C., & Rajan, S. (2011). Sri Lankan Tamil Refugees in India: Rehabilitation mechanisms, livelihood strategies, and lasting solutions. *Refugee Survey Quarterly, 30*, 24–44.

Zagarell, A. (1997). The megalithic graves of the Nilgiri Hills and The Moyar Ditch. In P. Hockings (Ed.), *Blue mountains revisited: Cultural studies on the Nilgiri hills* (pp. 23–73). New Delhi, India: Oxford University Press.

Conclusion

Abstract The final chapter concludes the monograph with a summary of its key findings followed by a consideration of their limitations as well as directions for future studies. In addition, there is a reflection on the methodology and epistemology of the research, and the author's position regarding the cultures it attempts to capture. The people studied in this book—rural-to-urban migrants in Bangalore, and Internet users in a virtual forum—were rich sources of information about Badagas living in India today and their encounters with new modes of sociality and quality of life. Although previous studies document a rich culture and history of Badagas, they are established on data, style, and trends of writers in the nineteenth century onwards, and underpin a simplified picture in need of updating. This multi-sited ethnography informs a critical update. It develops a revisionist narrative which, at an empirical level, unpacks ways migrants and netizens negotiate self and life quality while navigating inevitable shifts taking place in society and the circumstances in which they live; and, at a theoretical level, rebalances inequalities in representations of Badagas in the literature through revealing their lives in the twenty-first century as multiply-situated, dynamic, and fully engaged with modernity.

Keywords Badagas · Identity · Nilgiri Hills · Quality of life

There is no doubt that Badagas are living in truely momentous times. Migration to urban areas and overseas, and the dramatic rise of technologies such as new media, based on broader transformation of Indian society, have profoundly shaped people's cultures and lives. Badagas, like everyone in India, are experiencing new ideas and ways of living, and they are questioning who they are, how they live, and what kinds of social groups they belong to. In the midst of these changes, new forms of identities and quality of life have come into being. The people studied in this book—rural-to-urban migrants in Bangalore, and Internet users in a virtual forum—were rich sources of information about living in India today and encounters with new modes of quality of life and sociality, an important case study of people's lives in contemporary India.

Although previous studies meticulously document a rich culture and quality of life of Badagas, they are established on the data, style, and trends of writers in the nineteenth century onwards, and underpin a simplified picture in need of updating.

G. Davey, *Quality of Life and Well-Being in an Indian Ethnic Community*,
SpringerBriefs in Well-Being and Quality of Life Research,
https://doi.org/10.1007/978-3-319-90662-1_5

This monograph furnishes new insights: At an empirical level, it unpacks the ways migrants and netizens negotiated self and life quality while navigating inevitable shifts taking place in society and the circumstances in which they lived; at a theoretical level, it deconstructs and also challenges the ways Badagas have been characterised in the literature, and rebalances inequalities in their representation. Being Badaga is thoroughly in flux, and contested and negotiated across multiple spaces, as the evolving local and global realities of the 21st century elicit fundamental changes in its meaning and expression, not only social mobility and new lifestyles but alternative notions of self-understanding. These are strong claims which essentially challenge established viewpoints and make significant contributions to social science generally, and thus the next sections begin with a summary of the key findings from which they are derived, and consider their limitations as well as directions for future research. In addition, there is a reflection on the methodology and epistemology of the research, and the author's position regarding the cultures it attempts to capture.

Being Badaga in India Today

The previous chapters analyse the portrayal of Badagas in the literature as a coherent identity and cultural category with a high quality of life. By critically analysing the historical formation of different representations by social actors and social and political contexts, the findings show that previous reports do not do justice to the diversity of ways people report being Badaga. Previous descriptions seem to be an artefact of 'othering' by Western colonists and scholars, hinging largely on notions of distinct and stereotypical groups of tribes and cultures in the Nilgiri Hills; commentary on their quality of life was similarly constructed in writings and academic conventions in the nineteenth and twentieth centuries. They may be thought of as existing in the minds of their beholders, and perceived in rather different terms by Badagas. This monograph provides a revisionist narrative of such knowledge generation to rebalance the ways people have been described. Moreover, whereas the literature emphasises objective aspects of life quality, notably economy and standard of living, the previous chapters furnished a rich array of information about subjective quality of life by taking account of people's own constructions of their circumstances, as the conditions of Badagas, whether or not they face difficult times, and any improvements needed, depend in part on what they actually think rather than only the views of academics.

In conclusion, it is instructive to summarise the key findings of the ethnography. What does it mean to be Badaga in India today, and is it any different to being another Indian in the Nilgiris, South India, or beyond? It is clear that 'Badaga' was an identity trademark used by people to distinguish themselves and others. When the migrants and forum members discussed its meanings, salient themes included being born in the Nilgiri Hills (although current or length of residence was not important), having ancestry and family, speaking Badagu, and folk beliefs and ideals which imbued direction for how they lived. These strands were tied together by a deep and personal sense of being Badaga, the essence of who one is, and an integral part of their psyche which they valued immensely. These connotations were emotive, invoking feelings of pride, worthiness, and admiration of the efforts and achievements of Badagas, yet also humbled by their perceived failures. Overall, being Badaga was considered a positive identification, morally superior to being another person, and a relatively better life choice. It played a key role in wellbeing and quality of life by imbuing the capacity to enjoy and make a way through life. Happiness was interpreted as something that one is rather than something one has, a view of looking spiritually inward and outward through contemplation and inner reflection rather than in material things which were regarded as illusionary and transient. The good life was embedded in social relationships with family, and villagers, as everyone in surrounding areas knew and cared about each other. Thus, being an affiliate of the Badaga community in the Nilgiri Hills was important for a fulfilling and satisfying life. Indeed, they talked about 'collective happiness', a shared and combined sense of the wellbeing of Badagas as a whole and the general mood of the community, a collaboration among everyone working together for the common good. Individual wellbeing was said to stem from this social footing, as to be happy involved the happiness of others. Another major cord of the good life was a relationship with God, and doing good in life according to morals, as they believed a life of contentment and peace fitted into place for those who genuinely respected others and did good deeds; living well was seen as an outcome of the totality of their actions. Thus the findings shed light on the meanings of the good life from the perspectives of Badagas.

Resting on a common background, however, were diverse and conflicting thoughts about being Badaga, sometimes based on context-dependent and shifting criteria, and open to interpretation. Indeed, Chapter "Migrants' Voices" reveals a multiplicity of Badaga identities and their development and internalization which was an ongoing process of change over time. Thus, being Badaga is pluristic, flexible, and nuanced in multiple spaces, and not established automatically on the simple criteria (ancestory, language, locality, and so forth) documented in previous studies; while the category has been portrayed as straightforward and coherent in previous research, this monograph reveals ambiguities and complexities inherent in its construction and expression. Taking language as an example, the literature simply describes Badagas as people who speak Badagu, whereas in reality some people have limited knowledge of the language, city residents tend to communicate and conduct matters only in English and Tamil, some rural residents apparently use English and Tamil rather than Badagu to imply they live modern lifestyles, and young people in the Nilgiri Hills focus on fluency in English to improve their employment prospects in India and abroad. Second-generation migrants rarely conversed in Badagu even though it was regarded as their mother-tongue and played an important role in their lives as the language for expression of inner feelings and thoughts. Indeed, second-generation migrants cannot be characterised by many of the criteria which have been described as making up the identity category (reviewed in Chapter "Introduction"), and yet they regard themselves as Badagas and members of a community in the Nilgiri Hills. Another example is the finding that first-generation migrants purposefully shifted between Badaga identities in different contexts. In Bangalore they self-identified as City Badaga, an identity commitment among Badagas with migration experiences and assimilation of urban culture and lifestyle, an alternative to the supposed identities of Badagas in the Nilgiris or Bangaloreans in the city. Similarly, Chapter "Badagas Going Digital" shows communication on the Internet was an important means through which people negotiated and reinvigorated Badaga identities, as tensions and debates in the online forum showed that being Badaga was the object of intense contestation with multiple perspectives which people defended and contested. The Internet forum is also an example of a new type of Badaga social collective, a virtual community connected by notions of online culture, as new technologies have reshaped sociality and self as well as pathways for collective mobilisation to improve quality of life. Badagas dispersed in India and overseas use social media for communication with each other across geographical spaces, making it a common platform for identity making in ways that have never been possible in non-digital media. Therefore, social practices and identities among Badagas are changing as online spaces become more important and influence how they communicate and build groups of people no longer bounded by time and space.

The means by which identity change takes place, especially among ethnic minorities in India, is unclear in the literature. The findings in this monograph offer an analysis of specific processes, contextual determinants, and yardsticks involved in identity construction among Badagas. They show how City Badagas and Internet forum users became members of micro-cultures as they negotiated new aspects of their identities through reworking self and life, alternative ways of being Badaga in the city and online over and against prevailing meanings which led to cultural change and new formulations of self—identities as dynamic performantive structures in social action when people negotiate self. Also, while City Badaga and Nilgiri Badaga were described by interviewees as opposites, and urban and rural cultures and lifestyles turned into a site of differentiation, based on beliefs about the sort of person one is and should be in Bangalore or the Nilgiris respectively, they were actually mutually constitutive. For example, both identity orientations were acted out by the same person as a negotiation with social context to regulate the type of Badaga they thought they needed to be to fit in and uphold social accord. They professed fairly positive views of their multiple identities and heritage and host cultures rather than regarding one as superior or inferior, and they did not distance themselves from the past to secure the present, as the idea of being Badaga—City Badaga, Nilgiri Badaga, or other—was a positive and powerful sense of belonging and connection. The migrants declined to make a binary choice of identifying solely with rural or urban, which could have led to problematic trajectories in their lives and wellbeing, and instead they constructed flexible identities. As identity change rested on continuity of existing identity elements compatible with new ones honed in new settings, the migrants managed to maintain a strong sense of being Badaga while concurrently adjusting to and incorporating features of urban life, and so it was both persistent and changeable. Put simply, the migrants in Bangalore were upholding their Badaganess while responding to the upheaval of leaving the Nilgiris and living in the city; and, similarly, the Internet forum users, as Badagas in urban areas outside the Nilgiris, were maintaining similar allegiances while also creating new online and urban ways of being Badaga. It is interesting to note that while identity processes identified in the forum and real life were fluid and malleable, identity flexibility seemed more salient in Bangalore. Perhaps the ability to be anonymous on the forum meant they were able to express and play out their views without the same kinds of fears that existed in the face-to-face world, as an anonymous forum member could simply avoid or ignore any negative reactions. Faced with more freedom to experiment with identity, forum users were perhaps less concerned about how other people reacted to their disobedience of stereotypical customs and lifestyles, unlike the migrants who adopted identity flexibility to conform with others and appear 'normal' to mitigate negative reactions from others. The reporting of these identity processes builds on previous scholarship; and, while they are likely to be similar to the universal story of migrants, emphasises interaction among Badagas in the city, a unique relationship between self and society.

Claims that Badaga identities are manifold and in perpetual indeterminacy is perhaps dampened by stubbornness in the literature of the simplistic reification of a Badaga category based on stereotypical criteria (e.g. birthplace, kinship, language, locality, and political mobilisation efforts), the common sense and popular notion of a group of people who hail from a particular region of India, speak a particular language, and behave a particular way. Despite apparent problems in constructing such a category, it seems to be universally accepted by previous writers. However, its persistence relies more on how others have been observed through a Western-centric lens, first in European exploration of the New World and colonialist discourse and then academic reporting, as explained in Chapter "Introduction". These ideas were uncritically adopted and reinscribed by early intellectuals who gave a false appearance of coherence to identities and quality of life in their descriptions of distinct primitive societies in a microcosm (Nilgiri Hills) isolated from the South Indian majority, tied up with cultural relativism; that is, Badagas as a homogenous, spatially-bound, and distinct rural community of about 160,000 people with certain proxy measures such as cultural and historical traits framed in terms of similarity or otherness. Racist subcultures and institutional racism made such imagery—claims to the identities and improved living conditions of dark-skinned 'savages' by colonists and anthropologists, pivoted around articulations of power and difference, race, gender, and class—acceptable and seemingly natural, the very conditions which helped to legitimate their roles in India by socially constructing a positive image of themselves vis-à-vis the 'other' through a Western-centric lens. To some extent, Badagas self-identify with such notions, as interpretations by the migrants and online forum members depended to some extent on shared common attributes, buttressed by the ways most people tend to think of human culture and space as distributed in neat and tidy spatially-bound entities with markers corresponding to group divisions. Ironically, the simple Western-assigned cognitive categories, objective and impersonal, have come to be perceived as officially-constituted, even by Badagas themselves, which partly explains some of their beliefs reported in the interviews and forum posts, despite origins in historical discriminatory practices. However, people also gave diverse opinions about being Badaga which challenge the basic assumptions of a coherent category. Whereas previous writings follow a categorical model of description, my findings show that people should instead be viewed dimensionally. In other words, any perceived differences among ethnic minorities in the Nilgiris (or with others in South India) have conventionally been seen in terms of type of criteria rather than degrees of similarity or difference on a scale within the same criteria. Rather than previous approaches which look at Badagas categorically—you are either a Badaga or not—it is more accurate to look at people in terms of scale degrees or dimensions. While there are advantages to using a categorical model, the most important being convenience, the simplification creates problems, as discussed in Chapter "Introduction". One problem is that scholars have come to reify groups and view these social constructions as real things, whereas in reality everyone is the same except for a few variants of some aspects of culture. The categorisations in the literature often rely heavily on the impressions of individual writers. My reading of the literature actually suggests that people in these groups typically meet the diagnostic criteria of several groups. Thus I advocate for an alternative dimensional perspective in which people are not categorised or portrayed as different groups but instead rated on a series of cultural dimensions of the habits that most South Indians experience. Such a model would avoid the often arbitrary decisions which have been made in the literature in assigning people to certain markers or categories even though their differences are subtle and do not significantly differ from the Indian majority. It remains to be seen how the alternative model will be used in the future.

In conclusion, the label 'Badaga' is fixed in name only, as it seems to be primarily a process of being and becoming, open to negotiation with moment and context, and reflective of human experience in the many ways it is lived, and not a fixed entity reduced to simple criteria (and, for all their imagined distinctiveness, Badagas follow a familiar Indian pattern). Beneath the surface of simple definitions of the category 'Badaga' is diversity, vagueness, and contestation which show that people do not conform to the model of a closed and sealed tribal society and customary cultural prescriptions. This revisionist narrative can be regarded as a challenge to the rigid and stable identity constructions in the literature which seem to be largely a Euro-American invention. In this ethnography, Badagas played an active role in unpacking interpretations around which they organised their identities and quality of life, a more personal evaluation than previous research which only echoed the views of colonists and early academics and their objective and stereotypical categories of description. Rather than consider Badagas from the top down, which essentially portrays them as puppets controlled by the strings of macro-level institutions and social structures, this monograph shifts focus to micro-level processes and conceives people as agentic and integral in creating their social world, a bottom up approach focused on their subjective viewpoints and making sense of the world, and the multiplicity of Badaga life journeys. The findings also dispel the prevailing perspective of the Nilgiris as an isolated cultural enclave of hill tribes, even though it is repeated in current writings (e.g. Nielson and Pritchard 2009; Hockings 2013). My analysis also shows there are serious consequences of spreading such stereotypical and racialized knowledge construction in the West to non-Western cultures. Even so, despite substantial disagreement over the specifics of being Badaga, and identity change among those who went to the city and Internet forum, the all-encompassing Badaganess remained. For example, the words 'City Badaga' symbolise a linkage of the individual, Nilgiris, and Bangalore. Although the qualifier 'City' implies difference, the signifier 'Badaga' assumes continuity and commonality (and 'Badaga' alone, whatever its meaning, was sufficient to align with everyone in the group). Thus diverse Badaga identities were nested on images of a vague common background which served as an anchor, although they varied among people considerably.

The findings also explain the notions in the literature (Mandelbaum 1982; Hockings 1999) of a 'successful', 'powerful' and 'wealthy' South Indian community as Western academic discourse reminiscent of the cultural, economic, and political aspirations of British and American writers. They positioned the changed way of life in the Nilgiri Hills after the arrival of colonists as superior to the past, as if colonialism is what past and present is all about. Temporal comparisons in the interviews and forum posts of recent and dated living conditions (notably the 1990s when availability of employment, and high incomes from tea cultivation, provided a comparatively higher standard of living) show that quality of life has declined for Badagas. Unfortunately, a salient theme in both studies of the ethnography was a bleak situation in the Nilgiris as farmers made barely enough money to survive, and some tea gardens were financially unviable. Their livelihoods were characterised as low incomes and living standards, debts, unemployment, limited opportunities, and out-migration to nearby cities. There was emphasis in the Internet forum on the vulnerable position of farmers in the tea industry in which the overwhelming proportion of economic returns flowed to other stakeholders. Other aspects of low life quality in the Nilgiris, as revealed in the findings, included education, healthcare, and infrastructure. The participants also noted marked socioeconomic inequalities between the Nilgiris and cities, and between and within villages. My own observations confirm homes have basic amenities for living, but the findings reported in Chapter "Badagas Going Digital" reveal some people have inadequate conditions, especially in remote areas, and that quality of life at the village level matters, a direction for future research. The unfortunate reality was an appreciable number of people struggling for satisfactory living resources. In contrast, the migrants painted a more rosy picture of life in Bangalore, particularly with employment, income, convenient-living, access to education, and notions of social mobility and personal growth, albeit balanced with a downside to city life. Although the migrants and forum members noted many positive aspects of quality of life in the Nilgiris (for example in a social comparison with rural people in Indian States perceived to be worse off economically), these comparisons seem simple considering the wide range of relative standards evaluations past and present, and further research is needed. Overall, then, the Badagas I studied gave a different perspective to that of the success, progressive attitudes, and openness to change portrayed in the literature (Hockings 1999), as there was a consensus that people were experiencing hardships, had missed opportunities over the years, and struggled to adapt to changing India.

Intersections of Quality of Life, Identity, and Migration

Migration and city living were emotionally challenging at times, especially when the men relocated and adjusted to the new environment and changing perspectives of self. However, only a minority experienced a major struggle. Judging from their relatively healthy adjustment to the city, it could be argued identity flexibility served the migrants well as a novel avenue to express a new autonomy in the city while maintaining connectedness to family and native culture in the Nilgiri Hills, in other words a buffer of potential disruption, although doing so was a careful balancing act and not risk-free. Rural-to-urban migration was viewed positively by the participants as a vehicle of personal growth, a changed view of self and others which came out of experimenting with new ways of thinking and making sense of life. Also, the shared affiliation with the city (City Badaga) nurtured friendship and support among migrants, as association with each other as a social group was a common space they occupied as Badagas outside the Nilgiris (as was sociality in the Internet forum which connected people otherwise separated geographically and socially), a powerful emotional resonance of unity with others by feeling that they were not alone—a unifying force for a Badaga diaspora. This seems crucial for people marginalized outside their community, as the migrants and online forum members described difficulties connecting with Badagas. Thus affiliation among City Badagas or in a forum connected dispersed people, and facilitated identity-promoting activities such as friendship networks, social gatherings, and political action in which they fostered allegiances among themselves and with the community in the Nilgiri Hills. Membership of City Badaga also reassured the migrants when they experimented with the new ways of being in the city, and validated their legitimacy.

Identity served as the basis of cooperation to improve quality of life. The migrants in Bangalore desired to advance the standing of Badagas, taken a step further by forum members who worked together to bring about improvement. Also, the analysis of the forum seems to support the notion that people who communicate online tend to be more involved in local communities. Dissemination and debate of information in the forum enabled Badagas to express their fears and concerns, and provided a platform for awakening political consciousness to express different political views. Importantly, a new pathway to development was identified, as the forum was utilised for discussion of social and political issues as well as e-activism and e-philanthropy, examples of how Badagas improved their lives with technology. It is important because they face many challenges which existing circumstances in their current form have been unable to address. How they deal with these over the coming decade will significantly impact their life quality and future. These linkages of identities and life quality concur with research in a number of academic disciplines which positions identity as central to social capital and health and well-being.

It is instructive to consider claims that new media can improve quality of life in India, a country currently busy constructing the necessary technology infrastructure to meet the needs of its population. Digital and new media have fundamentally altered the ways people live, and a voluminous literature discusses their negative and positive implications. Regarding Badagas, previous studies documented radio and television consumption (Hockings 1999). This monograph is the first look at the potential of new media to shape their culture and lives in the coming years. Taking the findings as a record of an early Internet experiment among Badagas, they can be regarded as a starting point to ponder the future. Society could even be at the dawn of a new era as people take advantage of breakthroughs in technology that fundamentally change the ways they live. But can the case study be scaled up to address poverty and social deprivation? Although it remains an open question, it is important to reflect on possible scenarios. The Internet as a technology of communication afforded Badagas with access to knowledge and debates about quality of life issues that mattered most. It can be scaled-up to empower them to discover and disseminate information to improve their lives, for example to operate agricultural systems more efficiently, and secure alternative ways of living, as the findings revealed an inadequate response to changing economic and societal circumstances. For example, agriculturalists can use the Internet to access timely and location-specific information about market prices, farming techniques, innovation and best practice, and weather updates—a step towards precision agriculture which relies on timely information via new technologies to optimise business. Mobile telephony is increasingly being utilised by farmers in India to obtain real-time news and advice regarding agricultural commodities, markets, and weather updates. A number of studies have examined its impact on agricultural outcomes and rural livelihoods, although not in the Nilgiris. It is also important to consider the advocacy aspirations of the migrants and Internet forum users. Chapter "Badagas Going Digital" reveals a novel form of activism by Badagas (e-activism) not documented previously, and so it is clear that the Internet is changing their ability to engage in political organizing. Importantly, it empowered them to form alliances and work together across geographical boundaries to raise awareness of issues, propose and discuss solutions, and coordinate and take action to improve quality of life. Such rhetoric also puts a different spin on their circumstances as their desire for change evokes a sense of opportunity, and replaces the portrayal in the forum of Badagas as victims with notions of empowerment and positivity.

For these reasons, the e-activism in the forum should be considered further. The accuracy of claims by some forum members of price-fixing and unethical money lending in the tea industry was not verified with evidence, and difficult to evaluate without further investigation. Yet they seem to concur with Bhowmik's (1997) report of exploitation by tea factories and agents in the Nilgiris. Factory owners were alleged to have collaborated in price fixing to avoid competition with each other, and farmers had no bargaining power; the agents were regarded as primarily responsible for the low prices farmers received. Bhowmik (1997) also found farmers preferred to supply tea leaves to factories which provided interest-free loans for agricultural development, and in return the factories expected a regular supply from the farmers until the loan was repaid in full. Although some farmers had formed cooperatives to ensure fair prices, corruption and favouritism by management were reported. Bhowmik (1997) also noted studies undertaken by the Tea Board showed factories exploited small farmers. However, stakeholders in the Nilgiri tea industry have dismissed the allegations, and counter-claimed their activities were monitored by committees and the

Government (Neilson and Pritchard 2009). Therefore, further research and action is needed to investigate these issues raised in the forum. When considering the activists' claims, it should be noted the tea industry was more complex than its depiction in the forum, and they were not experts of the tea industry or the law. The business chain described by forum members is very simple when compared to an academic analysis by Neilson and Pritchard (2009) which described a complex system of more than 60,000 smallholders, 40 large tea farms, and agents, brokers, factories (bought-leaf, cooperative, estate), public auction centres in Coonoor, Coimbatore, and Kochi, as well as blenders, distributors, exporters, retailers, and wholesalers. The authors also situated the system in a complex interplay of institutions and governance in local to global cultural, economic, and political spheres. In addition to overlooking complexity, Badagas writing in the forum misunderstood some aspects of the business chain. For example, a post which alleged farmers were exploited by price manipulation because prices of tea sold by retailers were much higher than prices paid to farmers shows ignorance of the process of adding value to products during business chains which is eventually passed on to the end consumer (a series of business processes including manufacturing, packaging, branding, and retailing, which all cost money). Other aspects of the activism was misdirected, for example emails sent to the Central Bureau of Investigation (CBI) to raise awareness of issues affecting Badagas, even though it is the Indian government's national security and intelligence agency which investigates serious crimes. Also, the negativity of farmer versus agent narratives in the forum overlooked positive aspects as well as the fact that some farmers with smallholdings also act as agents. For example, agents provide farmers with access to national and international markets, and tea buyers with access to a wide variety of sellers, and help to peg prices to market conditions. It should be noted that crop prices and agents are not new issues for Badagas; for example, the prices of grain they sold in British India were fixed, fluctuated yearly, and were affected by grain surplus in nearby 'lowland markets' (Hockings 1980; Raju 1941). In the period between the two world wars, many Badagas with small land-holdings experienced difficult times and debts, and some sold land to non-Badagas to pay off outstanding debts (Thurston and Rangachari 1909; Ranga 1934). Some of these issues resonate with those reported in the Internet forum, and therefore should be considered in a historical context. In conclusion, I am not satisfied that prima facie was established in the allegations written in the forum. The activists also exaggerated the level of justification and support for their cause.

E-philanthropy in the Internet forum linked donors and recipients across national and international borders, and enabled small-scale donors to contribute funds to charitable projects easily without going through financial intermediaries and banks, a kind of Badaga-to-Badaga microfinance. The e-philanthropy could be harnessed further to support those in poverty, as the interviews and forum discussions implied some people in the Nilgiris had insufficient funds to mitigate daily living. The Internet forum could be enhanced with microfinance functions to develop credit models, verify borrower identity, and process payments between borrowers and lenders, and e-business initiatives could also be developed. Even so, it should be noted the suggestions above are underlined by technological determinism. When new media become more accessible and prevalent, it is up to Badagas to decide if and how they will be utilised, and what type of change, if any, will take place, as they will be the ones bringing it about. Though a causal relationship with development exists, it is complex and different in different contexts, and shaped by an array of factors including its social construction; in any case, there are varying ideas in development studies concerning what constitutes desirable change for a particular society. Thus, it is important to keep an open and technocultural mind whereby culture and technology intertwine in complex ways.

The proposition that new media could bring about material and social advancement of Badagas can also be challenged in other respects. The Nilgiri Hills, like India as a nation, is far from becoming a digital and information society, and online knowledge creation and distribution is not yet a dominant cultural and economic activity for the majority of the population. Badagas are currently on the wrong side of the Digital Divide, separated from the educated and urban elite which represent the majority of Internet users, a reflection of disparities in economic and social resources. New media are constrained in the Nilgiri Hills by inadequate telecommunication systems, high costs of technology, limited media ownership, and restrictive government policies. Resources are needed for technology to become a quality-of-life toolkit for Badagas, and the first step is to increase its availability and then identify mechanisms and pathways to embrace a technology-oriented future. Computers, 3G/4G technology mobile telephones, PDAs, and other devices are still relatively uncommon. The online community investigated in Chapter "Badagas Going Digital" does at least characterize the beginnings of a network society, and thus Badagas have definitely begun their journey on this path. Also, the digital divide is shrinking in India.

From Othering to Self-Othering

Reflexivity was an important component of the research, and took two main directions. First, research design and theoretical concerns were carefully considered, a quality control check. Second, the assumptions of the researcher were explored, a reflexive positioning of self and otherness to uncover any bias, inform interpretations of the findings, and make the research process itself a focus of inquiry. Thus reflexivity facilitated scrutinization of both the phenomena under study and research design by helping to situate oneself in the findings, and to be cognizant of personal history of the researcher and its influence (Alvesson and Sköldberg 2009; Woolgar 1988). From a symbolic interactionist vantage point, reflexive thinking enabled a consideration of the extent to which the researcher and researched co-produced the objects under study as a social construction. Meanings such as Badagas, quality of life, identities, and so forth, are not inherent but products shaped by the social worlds of the participants and researcher, and therefore it is important to reflect on the social construction of knowledge. As a white British anthropologist, the researcher began the ethnography with self-consciousness of potential cultural distance between the participants and himself, as the identity category has been harshly criticised for misrepresentations, researcher privilege, and power distance in the past which enabled studies of the Nilgiris by foreigners at the expense of what colonialism did to its population and environment (Misra 1999). As an insider is not necessarily a member of a group but someone who possesses intimate knowledge of it, data collection was preceded with extensive preparatory work including literature reviewing and trips and pilot work in Bangalore and the Nilgiris. I lived with Badagas to learn more about their lives, and to explore potential areas of enquiry and appropriate approaches. Sensitivity and respect were key ingredients in meeting and listening to people, analysing their words and worldviews, and nurturing empathy to represent them as accurately as possible; and the research process was open-ended, flexible, and highly dependent on their own preferences. The meanings of being Badaga were broached loosely, and not defined by the researcher, as participants were given freedom to convey their thoughts as they chose. Minimal constraint and informal procedures encouraged authentic voices, and enabled the participants to be involved in the direction of the research. The informal and relaxed nature of our interaction meant that any perceived distance was minimised.

As identities are inherently complex and fluid, the researcher can never be absolutely inside or outside those of the participants regardless of whether he is a Badaga or not. Caste and ethnicity are not the only relevant social signifiers of difference, as people have multiple and cross-cutting identifications, for example age, education background, employment status, sexuality, and other dimensions, not one continuum but a multiple series. Concordance of several criteria might be counterbalanced by discordance of others; for example, being a migrant, and an active participant on the Internet, as well as having other similarities with some of the participants. Consideration of such similarities and differences between the researcher and participants—elements of being inside on some dimensions and outside on others—was of considerable value in knowledge production. Being an outsider in some respects also made it possible to stand back to reflect on the full scope of the findings, to enable some objectivity towards producing better, less distorted research accounts. While reflexive steps taken could not lead to the perfect research interview (which in reality does not exist), acknowledging and working through these challenges enriched data collection and interpretation, and made assumptions and biases more manageable.

The symbolic interactionist approach of the monograph, although employed to overcome limitations of previous work, is not without criticism. A major critique is its ambiguous and impressionistic approach, as objects are interpreted differently by different people. As symbolic interactionism focuses on individual agency and informality, it may be less attuned to understanding larger groups and macro-level structures such as caste, class, economy, ethnicity, and historical circumstances, an ignorance perhaps of the extent to which humans inhabit a world not all of their own making (Goffman 1974). Similarly, if identity is subjective, constantly reinterpreted among individuals, and tied to time and context (Mead 1934), it may be reinterpreted by participants as they continue to adapt to the city and new media. Therefore, continuing the research, perhaps longitudinally, is suggested. Also, the sample interviewed in Bangalore does not represent all Badagas in urban areas. Experiences of migration could vary among individuals with different backgrounds and characteristics; other samples of interviewees (for instance, without a college education, working in low-paying manual jobs) might reveal different findings and a multiplicity of urban Badaga identities. As the sample consisted primarily of Gauda Badagas, the numerically dominant section of the population, and almost all of the participants were Saivite Hindus, further research can explore demographic diversity and its connections to quality of life and identities. It is also important to note migrants tend to represent a select group of people that leave their native place to pursue opportunities in a new society, and might be more motivated than the general population to embrace change, so it is not certain the findings will generalise to non-migrants. Similarly, focus on only one Internet forum narrowed the scope of the ethnography, and future research could investigate other online collectivities as well as social media.

Parting Thoughts

Interwoven into the monograph are threads of continuity and change. As the first in-depth investigation of the human and social experience of being Badaga, it examines the intricacies of quality of life and identity as an ethnic minority questioned and experimented with their place in contemporary India. Badagas expressed concerns about their future, the declining popularity of customs, and increasing outmigration to urban areas, and some even feared their community in the Nilgiri Hills was sliding to extinction. Discourses of decline and hardship are perhaps not surprising in the context of recent issues affecting the tea industry and national and global economies, a predominantly neoliberal economic standpoint. However, based on the key findings of the research, the view that Badagas are subjects of accelerating encroachment of globalisation and modernity should be considered with a good deal of scepticism. Pessimists should reflect on the findings which show that people are not subjects but participants, and not reified as groups set in stone but a work in progress in response to changing cultural and social context. Being Badaga actually reflects a process of being and becoming, and the many ways life is experienced, rather than a fixed entity reduced to simple criteria. Indeed, the findings debunk the myth in the literature that once upon a time there existed an undisturbed and fragile autonomous, distinct, and local Badaga community with well-defined traits and connections with locality. While previous writers suggest it is possible to imagine such a unified cultural identity, the findngs of this book show how it is very limited in its usefulness and contradicts such a wide, complex, and contextual range of experiences. The transformations taking place in India and globally should be welcomed as a significant force in improving quality of life and creating and proliferating identities. The participants reported identity change was enriching and a necessary cultural innovation to live together in difference in a globalised world, and they were generally positive about their new lives and changing circumstances in Bangalore which they thought were beneficial, although opinion was more divided online with support and refutation.

The monograph constitutes a big epistemological step forward for 'Nilgiriology'. Questions about whether observed phenomena really constitute constructions by scholars writing in certain genres and academic fashions have hardly entered writings on the Nilgiris. Moreover, academic discourse bespeaks unity, as writers seem to be in agreement about the category 'Badaga', which itself is problematic. The critique in this monograph fragments the unity, and encourages appreciation of the diversity and nuances of being Indian. These issues are also applicable to writings about other people in the Nilgiri Hills and India which are similarly allied to particular kinds of comparative and empiricist approaches, and come across as much of the same reporting, essentially analogous descriptions applied as if they are cross-cultural and universal. It is as if the authors had to organise their work in a similar fashion to describe principles and laws of operation presumed applicable to all societies, perhaps for their work to be accepted as ethnography. Furthermore, the new types of ethnographic research employed in this monograph, multi-sited and virtual ethnography, enriched with symbolic interactionism, are essential for understanding the intricacies of people's lives which cannot be captured by previous single-site ethnographic approaches (Davey 2008, 2012; Falzon 2009; Marcus 2011). Migration and new media also necessitate a re-think of how people live together, as life in the city and online are alternative socialities which challenge previous studies of Badaga culture and society.

The final line of thought I would like to take up briefly is the ethnography's broader implications as an important case study of people's experiences of contemporary India. The research shows quality of life and identity represent fascinating sites for examining how broader social trends in India and further afield are negotiated at the local level by ethnic minorities. At a societal level the findings reflect India's so-called economic development and integration into the global economy which has led to a capitalist society and rising popularity of cultural and material products of the West. One of the underlying tenets of multi-sited ethnography is to combine local practices with the national and global world system, and the findings trace Badagas across different spatial and cultural contexts and the kinds of global connections they are making between locales and larger social structures. While the analysis in preceding chapters relates specifically to Badagas, it also constructs a window through which to explore other ethnic minority people, and the extent to which change increasingly permeates self and quality of life, a more intimate picture of the impact of India's social and economic modernisation. Taking it a step further, the issue of what it means to be Badaga in India is ultimately about being Indian—the new City Badaga identity as a new Indianness shaped at the local level—and how it is constantly in flux, a pertinent concern at the forefront of debate about the future, not only in India but the world at large.

References

Alvesson, M., & Sköldberg, K. (2009). *Reflexive methodology: New vistas for qualitative research.* London, England: SAGE Publications.

Bhowmik, S. K. (1997). Participation and control: Study of a co-operative tea factory in the Nilgiris. *Economic and Political Weekly, 32*(39), A106–A113.

Davey, G. (2008). Twenty years of visual anthropology. *Visual Anthropology, 21*(3), 189–201.

Davey, G. (2012). Internet. In A. Stanton., E. Ramsamy., P. Seybolt., & C. Elliott (Eds.), *Cultural sociology of the Middle East, Asia, & Africa: An encyclopedia* (pp. IV228-IV230). Thousand Oaks, CA: SAGE Publications.

Falzon, M.-A. (Ed.). (2009). *Multi-sited ethnography: Theory, praxis and locality in contemporary research.* Surrey, England: Ashgate.

Goffman, E. (1974). *Frame analysis: An essay on the organization of experience.* Cambridge, MA: Harvard University Press.

Hockings, P. (1980). *Ancient Hindu refugees: Badaga social history, 1550–1975.* The Hague, The Netherlands: Mouton Publishers.

Hockings, P. (1999). *Kindreds of the earth: Badaga household structure and demography.* New Delhi, India: SAGE Publications.

Hockings, P. (2013). *So long a saga: Four centuries of Badaga social history.* New Delhi, India: Manohar.

Mandelbaum, D. G. (1982). The Nilgiris as a region. *Economic & Political Weekly, 17*(36), 1459–1467.

Marcus, G. E. (2011). Mulit-sited ethnography: Five or six things I know about it now. In S. Coleman & P. Von Hellermann (Eds.), *Problems and possibilities in the translocation of research methods.* London, England: Routledge.

Mead, G. H. (1934). *Mind, self, & society from the standpoint of a social behaviorist.* Chicago, IL: University of Chicago Press.

Misra, P. K. (1999, December 14). The Badaga way of life. *The Hindu.*

Neilson, J., & Pritchard, B. (2009). *Value chain struggles: Institutions and governance in the plantation districts of South India.* Sussex, England: Wiley.

Ranga, N. G. (1934). *The tribes of the Nilgiris: Their social and economic conditions.* Bezwada, India: Vani Press.

Raju, A. S. (1941). *Economic conditions in the Madras Presidency 1800–1850.* Madras, India: University of Madras.

Thurston, E., & Rangachari, K. (1909). *Castes and tribes of Southern India.* Madras, India: Government Press.

Woolgar, S. (Ed.). (1988). *Knowledge and reflexivity: New frontiers in the sociology of knowledge.* London, England: SAGE Publications.

Druck:
Canon Deutschland Business Services GmbH
im Auftrag der KNV-Gruppe
Ferdinand-Jühlke-Str. 7
99095 Erfurt